D0521567

Richard Harrington's ANTARCTIC

Richard Harrington's
ANTARCTIC

Cover—Adelie penguins hurl themselves into Hope Bay at the top of the Antarctic Peninsula. *Title page*—King penguins gossip in sonorous voices reminiscent of a trumpeter swan. *Below*—"The oakum boys," king penguin chicks. *Opposite*—King penguin rookery.

Copyright ©1976 Alaska Northwest Publishing Company, Anchorage, Alaska
All rights reserved. No part of this book may be reproduced or transmitted in any form or by any means, electronic or mechanical, including photocopying, recording or by any information storage and retrieval system, without written permission of Alaska Northwest Publishing Company.

Library of Congress Cataloging in Publication Data
Harrington, Richard, photographer.
    Richard Harrington's Antarctic.
    SUMMARY: Text and photographs portray the Antarctic continent and its surrounding islands including the Falklands, the South Orkneys, and Tierra del Fuego. Includes a chronology and the text of the Antarctic Treaty of December 1, 1959.
    1. Antarctic regions—Juvenile literature. [1. Antarctic regions] I. Title. II. Title: Antarctic.
G860.H26   919.8'9   75-43581
ISBN 0-88240-054-1

Designed by Roselyn Pape
CartoGraphics by Jon.Hersh
Alaska Northwest Publishing Company
Box 4-EEE, Anchorage, Alaska 99509
Printed in U.S.A.

Dedication

To Lars-Eric Lindblad, always eager to share his love of the Antarctic; to renowned ornithologist Roger Tory Peterson, ever patient with even the rankest of amateur bird watchers; to Captain Hasse Nilsson, who could sometimes bend a straight course a bit and thereby open fascinating new vistas, and Captain Rolf Nordell, unfailingly informative about navigation through pack ice—both are real ice men, able to handle a ship in any ice conditions; to Rolf Dornbach, thoughtful cabin companion on three antarctic voyages; and ultimately to all the penguins, seals and albatrosses who took us on trust and posed as exemplary models.

CONTENTS

Left—Penguin-shaped pack ice in the Ross Sea. *Right*—A Weddell seal sunning itself on the ice.

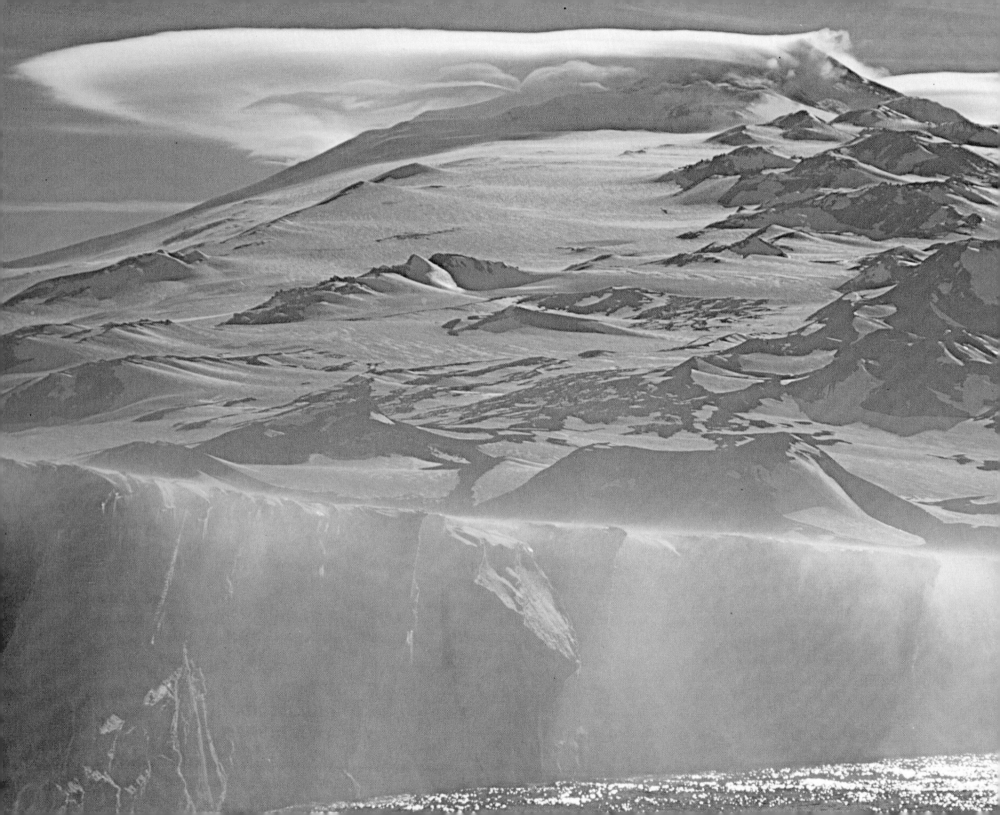

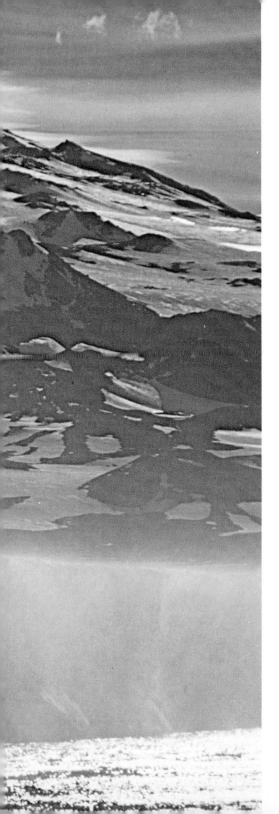

FOREWORD

Here is a book about the Antarctic and the Subantarctic, as seen by a Canadian photographer. Richard Harrington did not seek out scientific stations to report on their often-obtuse studies.

Rather it is a book of the great natural beauty, the wild magnificence of the Seventh Continent and its surrounding islands. The breath-taking splendor of a whole continent practically without human habitation. Where a man can observe wildlife that is unhunted and unafraid, wildlife that has adapted itself to the harsh antarctic climate.

Harrington has photographed in nearly every country in the world, not just once but often. I can safely say that he has captured many attractive phases of the Antarctic, which has drawn me on 13 visits. Like him, I feel that one can never see enough or experience enough of this still remote continent.

To some, the Antarctic might seem a barren, hostile land, but to the nature-lover, artist or any thoughtful individual, it is a region of endless surprise, change of light, sound, contours and experiences. This unique land and its peripheral islands should be preserved inviolate forever.

Roger Tory Peterson —

Thimphu, Bhutan, 1975

Opposite—The great Ross Ice Shelf, 197,000 square miles, is roughly four-fifths the size of Texas. The leading edge calves in tabular icebergs occasionally the size of Connecticut, and the fierce antarctic wind carves ice particles away. A high cloud at the peak seems like smoke, but Terror is an extinct volcano.

Rockhopper penguin.

RICHARD HARRINGTON'S FIRST VOYAGE

South Georgia

Atlantic Ocean

Falkland
Islands

South Orkney
Islands

Elephant Island

South
America

Antarctica

★
South Pole

Pacific Ocean

0   500   1000 Miles

Opposite—Two families share this small bay on West
Point Island in the Falklands. Fog can roll in at any time here.

The Friendly Falkland Islands

After distinguished exploration in the Arctic, where he had located the north magnetic pole, Sir James Clark Ross of the Royal Navy was directed by the Admiralty to locate its counterpart in the Antarctic.

Sir James didn't find the south magnetic pole, but in 1839 he discovered the immense Ross Ice Shelf, which a London newspaper blithely described as "the whitest, if not the brightest jewel in the British crown."

If the glittering diamond-hard continent may be considered a jewel, then each southern continent stretching toward it may be viewed as a claw of the setting.

Sir James approached the White Continent from Australia. Of my three visits to Antarctica, New Zealand was the springboard for my second voyage, and Tierra del Fuego for my third.

But I came first to Antarctica from the Falkland Islands, far south in the Atlantic Ocean.

A covey of 340 islands and islets, the Falklands have been a British possession since 1833. They are a bit of Old Scotland in appearance and lifestyle. The land area totals nearly

The Falklands have no trees, except those planted by man. Gentle hills often fall sheer to the sea, as here on New Island.

5,000 square miles and is laced with innumerable channels and fjords running back from the sea. Half the islands' meager population lives in the capital, Port Stanley.

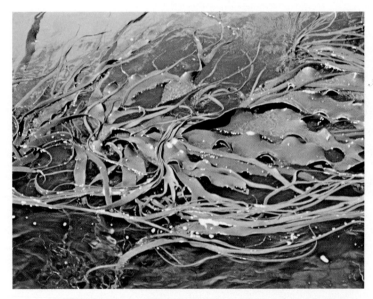

The kelp around the shores of the islands has a beauty of its own and is the basis of a small industry.

The neat town is not only the modest administration center for the islands, but the most important port for British supply ships serving the British Antarctic Survey stations and home port for the icebreaker HMS *Endurance*. In fact, here one gets the feeling that the direction of interest is south to the Seventh Continent.

The remaining 1,000 inhabitants live "in camp," a local corruption of *campos*, "countryside," along with 360,000 Polworth sheep. The islands' economy "rides on the woolly sheep's back."

The island-born are nicknamed "Kelpers," from the masses of seaweed that characterize their shores. Among them you are accepted without suspicion or hostility or phoniness. You feel at once a trusted friend. And crime is virtually unknown.

The wind blows constantly from the west, discouraging the growth of trees, but the blustery weather in no way limits the friendly warmth of the people. Walk along the few paved streets and residents will greet you with a cheerful "Good day" followed by an invitation to a cup of tea and a chat.

Waterfront of Port
Stanley, the only town in
the Falkland Islands.
Island vehicles are
mostly sturdy and practical.

13

An arch formed by whale ribs stands outside Christ Church Cathedral in Port Stanley. It was erected in 1933 to celebrate a century of British rule.

You walk through a fenced garden where alpine poppies nod their heads and spectacular lupines bloom in many delicate shades.

Sun porches, filled with geraniums and other flowering plants, face north to take full advantage of the sun. Invariably the homes are clean and snug, and old-fashioned, the parlor furniture drawn around a fireplace where a peat fire of turf cut from the hillside sends out a glow of warmth.

Port Stanley has a cozy little old-time hotel called the Blue Goose, where I was invited into the kitchen to sample a new batch of buns. A visitor need never be lonely in Port Stanley or anywhere in the Falklands.

Indeed my only problem was to extricate myself from such hospitality in order to visit the historic Christ Church Cathedral, the most imposing building in town, to look at the museum and gaze on old warehouses built from wrecked wooden ships. I wanted to stroll along the harbor, observe other wrecks and watch the shore birds. It all seemed to me like a pastoral scene from long ago.

14

Antarctica Compared to the Continental United States

And, of course, I visited the post office, for the Falklands and the entire Antarctic are rich hunting grounds for colorful stamps and interesting cancellations. While the islands' stamps honor the queen of England, those of Argentina show "Las Islas Malvinas," plus a narrow wedge reaching right down to the South Pole, as Argentine territory.

The Falkland Islanders are in a unique and difficult position, politically. Though everyone is of British descent, England is far away, and

The Falklands have abundant marine life along the shores, such as mussels, barnacles and kelp. The islands also have many summer wild flowers, including this dusty miller.

15

Cypress and flowering gorse provide a windbreak for sheep station homes. Sheep raising is almost the only industry in the islands, where the Polworth, below, is raised for its wool. Mutton is a staple food.

Argentina close at hand. Britain democratically insists on a plebiscite, someday, while Argentina constantly woos the Falklands, which it claims as part of the heritage it wrested from Spain.

Within deep windows curtained in starched lace, you may often read a sign: KEEP THE FALKLANDS BRITISH. But time and proximity may be on Argentina's side. The Kelpers' allegiance was tested recently by Argentine aid in building an airstrip and establishing an air link with

Most Falkland Islanders wish to remain British and not accept Argentina's territorial claims.

A sheep station on New Island provides homes for ranch hands. Though the ground is stony, the islands support more than 600,000 sheep. A wrecked interisland boat lies in the foreground.

Comodoro Rivadavia, the nearest Argentine port.

Some students from the Falklands now attend the British school in Buenos Aires, instead of going home to England. And many others are becoming bilingual, since most trade is carried on with Spanish-speaking Argentina.

The real life of the Falkland Islands is in camp, the countryside and offshore islands. Only 15 of the islands* are inhabited, but grazing sheep, seals and penguins share far more.

The sheep stations are like the *estancias* of Argentina, though much less feudal in outlook. Good homes are provided for the managers and chief shepherds, and comfortable small homes for the ranch hands and their families. The largest of the 39 stations sprawls over one and a third million acres. Its headquarters is a large village, complete with a boarding school.

Usually shepherd families live isolated lives, with only one or two families near. Invariably their houses are roofed with corrugated iron, usually

*West Falkland, East Falkland, Lafonia, Bleaker, Lively, Beaver, Carcass, New, Pebbles, Kepple, Saunders, Sea Lion, Speedwell Group, Weddell, West Point.

A baby elephant seal rests in the tussock grass.

Right—Many beaches in the islands are formed of jagged rocks, green with algae.

painted red or green, and surrounded with windbreaks of evergreen macrocarpa and hedges of fragrant yellow gorse.

Mail, including school lessons by correspondence, is dropped by interisland plane, and freight is brought by interisland steamer. Lambing and shearing are the busy times of the year, as on any sheep ranch. Neither the adults I met nor the children ever seemed bored or lonely. Any longing for cities is quickly satisfied. One intelligent, well-informed shepherd of 24 had never left the Falklands and had no craving for life beyond his islands.

I have seen returning students blink back tears of joy at sight of a bleak hillside where sheepdogs raced out in ecstatic welcome. Life in camp is good, they realize, and though the fare may be mutton every day, it is cooked deliciously in many ways. Our barbecue

on the beach of New Island was nothing novel to the cheerful residents.

Both in town and in camp, people know and treasure Nature—the unique birds such as the flightless steamer duck, or the Falkland Islands fur seal, or the groundsel that is a cabbage. Sperm and pilot whales still spout and strand themselves in shallows, and dolphins frolic in the countless channels. Seals—elephant, fur and leopard—are easily spotted, while sea lions prefer the safety of craggy islands.

The sea crashes against high cliffs, and the wind erodes them into caves, then stacks. The striated headlands rear high over sandy or bouldery beaches. My memory of the Falklands is one of blue sky and sea, the gold of gorse and sunshine, a scene almost Mediterranean.

Yet a golden day can quickly become blustery and overcast, and rain slash across the cropped pasture.

Above—Male fur seals guard harems and young on a flat rock ledge on New Island, where they are making a comeback. Kelp streams in the water beyond.

Left—Some beaches are deceptively balmy in sunshine, but the water is very cold. Sea birds, including penguins, haunt this fine sand beach fringed by gorse on Carcass Island.

19

The air was full of bird song as we tramped over Carcass Island. Sixty species of birds breed in the Falklands, and migrants stop here. Songbirds, petrels, the upland goose that is prized for Christmas dinner, five species of penguins—king, gentoo, Magellan, macaroni and rockhopper in descending size—squawk and gabble in their millions, ignoring human visitors.

We picked our way along the shore, keeping a lookout for holes the Magellan penguins had burrowed at the roots of the tussock grass. Bolder individuals thrust their heads out to see what all the tramping was about, and swiveled them around at impossible angles. A tussock bird tried to undo my shoelaces.

Ranchers used to persecute Magellan penguins because of the holes they tunneled. But conservationists proved that their burrowing and their droppings actually improved pasturage.

On New Island, the wind brought a stench across the pasture from a large rookery of gentoo penguins; the shepherd had fenced off the rookery to prevent the sheep from trampling the chicks. The gentoos' gabble rose in alarm when we approached, as adult penguins protected their two chicks from any harm we might cause. And they can give you a severe nip with those heavy beaks.

Our young guide informed us regretfully that usually one chick would prove the stronger and survive by getting most of the parents' food. Still, it was obvious that this rookery was not in decline since there were thousands of birds on the plain.

New and West Point Islands both boast rookeries of rockhopper penguins. These little fellows, red of eye and beak, have startling yellow eyebrows and feather topknots. It is amazing to watch half a million penguins using flippers and claws to jump and scramble up steep rocks to ledges well above the surf pounding against the base of the cliff.

Triangular West Point Island slopes from thousand-foot sandstone cliffs down to the settlement on shore. Part of the coast has steep cliffs of layered sandstone, part is sandy beach littered with whale bones and rusty whaling machinery. This island was for 200 years a favorite rendezvous for whalers and sealers.

Explorers and seamen of the Royal Navy made a practice of setting

A group of Magellan penguins troop seaward on New Island. On Carcass Island, a large, dark male sea lion guards his harem jealously.

Rockhopper penguins are known by their markings: red eyes and beak, yellow topknot and eyebrows.

Little remains of this whaling shore station on New Island except lichen-spotted machinery and bones. Nearby, a black-browed albatross sits on its egg in a nest of peat and tussock grass.

domestic livestock ashore to breed and multiply against possible future need. The animals ran wild, of course, and when sailors craved fresh meat instead of salted, it was there for the taking.

Later, owners of the land might take a dim view of what they considered trespass. In fact, the young United States of America nearly went to war with Britain over the right of New England sealers and whalers to help themselves on West Point Island. But then the Civil War intervened, and whaling soon swept farther south. ◄◄◄

Rounding King Edward Point into Cumberland Bay West, a white cross, memorial to Sir Ernest Shackleton, meets the eye. He died in 1922 at Grytviken, a mile across the bay. Saddle-peaked Mount Paget rises 9,825 feet above the whaling town.

The magnificent wandering albatross has an 11½-foot wing-span and spends nearly all its life soaring over the seas.

In Shackleton's Wake

The Falkland Islands, like Tierra del Fuego, are part of the great underwater extension of the Andes. Mountain peaks surface as islands in the curving Scotia Arc.

The arc also includes the South Orkney, the South Shetland and the South Sandwich groups, as well as the large island of South Georgia, which stretches its 100-mile length across longitudes 36° and 37° east some 800 miles southeast of the Falklands.

Though British for two centuries, all these islands are claimed by Argentina, in accordance with a papal edict of 1494 that divided New World discoveries between Spain and Portugal.

Around latitude 55° south, the Atlantic Ocean takes on a different character, and our bow plunged deep into waves. We had reached the Antarctic Convergence, and at once noticed the drop in temperature. The convergence corresponds to the tree line in the Arctic. Once past it, you are definitely in the polar zone.

It is a girdle of turbulent water 20 to 30 miles wide, where the heavy, cold antarctic currents meet and sink beneath the warmer water flowing south. The turbulence keeps the bottom roiled, providing good feeding for sea life.

South of the convergence the currents flow clockwise, rich in nitrates and phosphates that promote growth. The Atlantic, Pacific and Indian oceans combine in 12.5 million square miles of what is increasingly being called the Southern Ocean.

Far ahead, almost unseen under a lowering gray sky, we spotted a most isolated and dismal cluster of rocks: the Shag Rocks. Part of the Scotia Arc, they

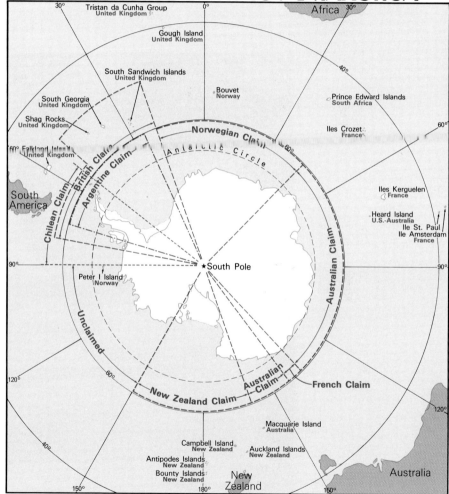

National Claims to Antarctica

Tristan da Cunha Group
United Kingdom

Africa

Gough Island
United Kingdom

South Sandwich Islands
United Kingdom

Bouvet
Norway

Prince Edward Islands
South Africa

South Georgia
United Kingdom

Iles Crozet
France

Shag Rocks
United Kingdom

Norwegian Claim

Falkland Islands
United Kingdom

Antarctic Circle

South America

British Claim
Argentine Claim
Chilean Claim

Iles Kerguelen
France

Heard Island
U.S.-Australia
Ile St. Paul
Ile Amsterdam
France

Australian Claim

★ South Pole

Peter I Island
Norway

Unclaimed

New Zealand Claim

Australian Claim

French Claim

Macquarie Island
Australia

Campbell Island
New Zealand

Auckland Islands
New Zealand

Antipodes Islands
New Zealand

Bounty Islands
New Zealand

New Zealand

Australia

23

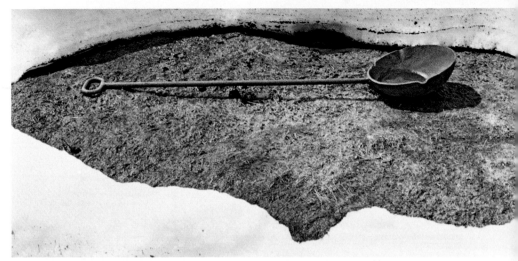

Receding snows at Grytviken reveal a 4-foot ladle that was used for testing when blubber was rendered in try pots on shore.

Young elephant seals loll in safety amid the rusting machinery at Grytviken. Once, whales, seals, even penguins went into the digesters to be rendered into oil.

rise sheer about 300 feet to the surface and almost that high above the water. It is unlikely that these rocks have ever been climbed, since they rise abruptly, with neither a spot to land nor anchorage for a ship. The ledges and crannies were jammed with nesting blue-eyed shags, and petrels came wheeling around our ship as we nosed in briefly.

These crags were labeled "disappearing islands," because having been reported in 1762, they couldn't be found again. It took until 1927 to pin them down correctly on a navigational chart.

Our first view of whale-shaped South Georgia was one of snow-capped mountains under low clouds. The humped spine rises to 9,825 feet in saddle-peaked Mount Paget. Width varies from 3 to 25 miles between the formidable south shore and the deep bays of the north coast.

Ravines were filled with glaciers slipping down to the Scotia Sea. It was almost as void of human presence as when Captain James Cook both named it and claimed it for his sovereign George III in January 1775. Cook thought the island hardly worth discovering. Perhaps it was too great a contrast to the Tahitian Islands he had just left. He wrote in his journal:

The wild rocks raised their lofty summits till they were lost in the clouds, and valleys lay covered with everlasting snow. Not a tree was to be seen, nor a shrub big enough to make a toothpick.

Then he added, "Seals or sea-bears were pretty numerous, for the shores swarmed with young cubs."

That comment brought the fur sealers and whalers in their multitudes from Scandinavia, the British Isles and the New England states. South Georgia became an important whaling center, with seven shore stations in operation in

From left—The bleak Shag Rocks rise sheer out of the Scotia Sea to about 300 feet, halfway between the Falklands and South Georgia. Mosses grow beautifully green in the glacial brooks of South Georgia. A Kerguelen fur seal drinks from a meltwater brook.

The main British Antarctic Survey station at King Edward Point, where the *John Biscoe* unloads at the dock. The 20 men live in Shackleton House, the large green building at left; they have a splendid view of South Georgia's 9,000-foot mountains.

Grytviken, once the whaling capital of the South Atlantic, is a 15-minute walk around Cumberland Bay West from the British survey station. Several whale-catchers are grounded at the derelict dock.

26

Left—Glacial meltwater courses through the whaling station at Grytviken and out this big pipe into the bay. A couple of elephant seals lounge on the grassy bank.

1915, when Sir Ernest Shackleton launched his third antarctic expedition.

As we turned into the commodious double Cumberland Bay, we sighted a white cross on a hillside close to the British Antarctic Survey station. It was a memorial to Shackleton, who had died in this harbor on the eve of his fourth antarctic expedition, in 1922. It was our first encounter with the Heroic Age of polar exploration.

Since the B.A.S. dock was occupied by the research ship *John Biscoe*, our cruise ship the *Lindblad Explorer* steamed on around the bay about a mile to where the abandoned whaling station of Grytviken suddenly met our eyes.

Brown, rusting, totally still, it waits silently for its end. A ghost town of empty homes and bunkhouses, offices and shops. Forgotten whale-catchers sit on the bottom of the harbor, leaning against the old dock.

Inch by inch we moved to the decrepit dock. Whaling no longer requires shore stations, only factory ships where the huge sea mammals are drawn up on the deck for the knives of the flensers and lemmers, before they reach the digesters and pressure cookers that render the oil.

The whaling station has not been used since the padlocks went on the doors at the close of the 1965 season. The machine shop that could repair large boats is silent, the tall chimneys smokeless. No sign of blood or guts stains the *plan* where the great animals were cut up. But an air of melancholy hangs about the place, as the pungent reek of whale oil lingers. More decades of harsh South Georgia weather will be needed to clean the black, greasy soot from the roofs.

We prowled around the town and peered through occasional windows.

The hulk of a wooden sailing ship was beached to form a breakwater for Grytviken. Elephant seals sport in the water, no longer hunted for their oil.

Transport costs are too high to bother with salvaging the scrap metal in these whale-catchers at Grytviken.

Even today a single switch will set a generator going, and a few lights will flicker on, powered by water impounded up the mountainside.

I walked across a deep, hard snowdrift to a grassy knoll where a few dandelions had rushed into bloom. Two old-time try pots and a couple of old-fashioned harpoons were mounted on permanent display in front of the deserted administration building. These pots, 3 feet in diameter, were relics of the oilers who rendered whale, seal or penguin oil on open beaches, souvenirs of the days of wooden ships.

I peered through clean windows into workshops and into a storage shed where thousands of new harpoon heads were stacked, never to be used.

Past the Kino, the cinema that doubled as a game room, past the steepled white church (now a recreation hall for the dozen men who winter at the British Antarctic research station across the bay), we skirted the fetid muck where dimwitted elephant seals pass their time in malodorous slumber.

Once in a while, men from the British station at King Edward Point visit the Grytviken cinema or church for some special occasion.

The footpath brought us to the tidiest corner of Grytviken, the little white-fenced cemetery. Among the wooden crosses sits a granite shaft, which reads:

To the dear memory of
ERNEST HENRY SHACKLETON
EXPLORER
Born Feb. 15, 1884
Died Jan. 5, 1922

He lies in the land he loved, and which he knew better than anyone else.

Shackleton spent the spring month of November 1915 here at Grytviken. He was leading the British Imperial Transantarctic Expedition, his third south polar journey. He planned to cross the Weddell Sea, then sledge to the South Pole, then north to McMurdo Sound.

Instead, his ship, the *Endurance*, was quickly seized by the pack ice, which carried it for 281 days before crushing it. Even so, it reached a lower latitude than any previous vessel.

Then and in the months they survived on floe ice, all 28 men continued their oceanographic work, working their way northward to Elephant Island in the South Shetlands. Shackleton left most of them on its inhospitable shore while he and five companions rowed and sailed a lifeboat across 800 miles of

Keith Shackleton, great-nephew of the explorer, and *Lindblad Explorer* Captain Hasse Nilsson place a wreath on Shackleton's grave.

stormy ocean to the nearest help, a whaling station on South Georgia.

When the leaky boat would carry them no farther, Shackleton and two of the men climbed the 9,000-foot mountain range, crossed it, and made a perilous descent to Stromness Bay on the north shore. With that kind of stamina, how could he fail to rescue his stranded crew?

Clumps of elephant seals lay outside the picket fence of the Grytviken cemetery. In fact, cows and young bulls lay everywhere on shore and in the shallows, like gargantuan slugs. They must complete their molt before they follow the bigger bulls back to the sea. Full-grown males reach up to 20 feet in length and 4 tons in weight. To human eyes they are ugly, but that droopy proboscis can inflate to magnificently amplify a roar.

At times, I walked up to the tail end of a dozing elephant seal and scratched the smooth brown or gray pelt. Some responded like a dog, scratching the same spot with a clawed flipper. If one bothered to waken, it would look dimly alarmed out of big, dark eyes, and promptly fall asleep again.

Or in a stinking wallow they might flop around, their sausagelike bodies lolling on the tufted grass. It is hard to believe that they are strong, alert

The *Lindblad Explorer* docks at Grytviken, rarely visited today. Beyond the old breakwater is the small white-fenced cemetery.

animals when in the water. Young bulls grunted, occasionally roared, or heaved vast sighs of foul breath. But these were only gestures, not serious threats. They might attack a human, but generally they back away.

A sailor with club or harpoon could easily drive a herd of them backward to a killing beach.

It is ironic that the defenseless animals have outlasted the bullyboys and their weapons. So I enjoyed seeing them draped over oil drums, or snoozing in perfect safety amid rusting cogwheels and pipes that are no longer a menace.

We had hoped to call in at Stromness Bay's whaling station, the terminus of Shackleton's amazing adventures on sea and land, but it is off-limits to all visitors because of vandalism. Who expected vandalism in Antarctica? Or ghost towns, for that matter?

Eastward from Grytviken we had also expected to visit Royal Bay with its colony of king penguins, but the waves were too violent. So we turned back toward the west end of the island.

Millions of sea birds nest on the island and islets of South Georgia. Our bird watchers identified most of the 28 species that breed there. These include five penguins—macaroni, chinstrap, king and gentoo (we didn't see the emperor, which visits only in winter to incubate on the ice); three albatrosses—wandering, black-browed and gray-mantled; four petrels—blue, storm, giant and pintado.

Now undisturbed, a bull elephant seal establishes territorial rights to a pile of abandoned oil drums, and a macaroni penguin turns its large egg on a nest of a few pebbles, sheltered by a clump of tussock grass.

A black-browed albatross takes advantage of an updraft to land at Elsehul Bay on South Georgia.

King penguins, second in size only to the emperors, show little fear of the visitors stepping out of their inflatable craft at the Bay of Isles on South Georgia.

There were also the black-browed mollymawk; the blue-eyed shag (really a brown-eyed cormorant with a band of blue outside the eye); and brown skuas and sheathbills, both predators in the penguin colonies. I also heard, to my amazement, the song of a lark, and thus met the titlark *Anthus antarcticus,* Antarctica's only songbird.

Five miles from the western tip of South Georgia lies the fabulous Bay of Isles, a naturalist's dream of delight. Glaciers crawl down to the water's edge, where kelp streams in the current in long ribbons or lies coiled like sea serpents in mats strong enough to support the weight of a bird watching for fish.

We made a wet landing on steep, wind-swept Albatross Island. Overhead winged the great white birds, returning here to mate after 2 years at sea.

With a rope and scrambling on all fours, a small group of passengers

puffed to the top. The cool wind was strong, fortunately for the albatrosses, which need it for landing and takeoff. We lay on mossy stones or perched on clumps of tussock grass, voyeurs spying on the love-making of these magnificent birds.

The wandering albatross is peerless, with a wingspan of up to 11½ feet, the largest in the world. It comes here every second year to breed. Tirelessly the big birds circumnavigate the Antarctic Continent, clockwise, rarely resting on land or sea. The stormier the weather, the better they soar, wing tips only an inch above the waves.

The tussock grass rippled in the wind on the small plateau, practically a private landing strip for sea birds. Hundreds of beautiful white females perched on high, cuplike nests, ready to lay or incubate the single large egg. We watched the males return, feet outstretched, to make a pinpoint landing on the nest or at once mount the female. Other mated couples greeted the return

A pair of wandering albatrosses go through neck-stretching, wing-flapping courtship rites before beginning work on a mounded nest of peat and grass for their single egg. The young albatross shown above, molting and still unable to fly, remains dependent on its parents.

In the foreground
of this king penguin rookery
at the Bay of Isles
are the downy young,
nicknamed "the
oakum boys" for their
resemblance to a
reel of caulking material.
Beyond, adults climb
the snowfield to nests
far above the beach.

The Bay of Isles king penguin rookery has standing room only for its thousands of inhabitants. The adults, like the individual at left, incubate the solitary egg on their feet under a flap of soft, feathered belly skin.

As the chicks begin to lose their down, the beautiful markings of orange and gold begin to show. This one will soon take to the sea.

with ecstatic display, neck-stretching, wing-beating, beak-clattering.

Going ashore on the main island of South Georgia past the seaweed snakes, between the glaciers, we were met on the beach by a curious welcome committee of king penguins. Not in the least incommoded by our arrival, they dove into the sea and flew away under the waves. Beyond the beach we climbed a slight rise and found ourselves on the rim of a nursery of 10,000 king penguins, adults and downy young crowded only flipper distance apart.

King penguins are my favorite of all 17 species, being the most colorful, and instead of squawking they honk melodiously like trumpeter swans.

Adults have the characteristic white shirt front and black formal tails. In addition, both male and female have brilliant orange ear patches and a wide golden collar. Either parent places the single egg on top of its black feet and lowers a fold of feathered belly skin over it. The incubating partner sits upright regally for weeks, changing position only when the mate arrives to spell off.

Both birds are kept terribly busy feeding the downy young, which rapidly grow as tall as their parents and seem much bulkier. Men in the days of wooden ships called young king penguins "the oakum boys," because they looked like perambulating reels of the oakum used for caulking decks.

35

The South Orkney Islands are known for dismal weather. Fogs are frequent among the high, snowy mountains and pack ice often prevents ships from making a landing.

From the Bay of Isles, I walked across the width of South Georgia to Elsehul Bay, a few miles west of Shackleton's crossing. It took me only half an hour to trudge a slippery way between man-high pedestals of tussock grass. I walked among slumbering fur seals, cautious not to waken them to action, though the worst that could happen would be a nip and a slip in the foul muck of a wallow.

Reaching the south coast I sat on a cliff, watching the petrels wheel and the rockhopper penguins climb. Sounds rose from the beach below, crowded with elephant and fur seals and chinstrap penguins.

Small battles broke out among young elephant seals. Crying, grunting, snorting, a couple would flounce toward one another and meet with a tremendous clap, smacking breast to breast. Inflated proboscises trembling, red mouths open, the young warriors reared backward, making themselves tall, and smacked together again. Eventually one would rear higher than

Small white crosses mark Signy Island's tiny cemetery of the British Antarctic Survey station. Molting young elephant seals sleep in the foreground. *Right*—Red-clad passengers from the cruise ship scatter around the station, where elephant seals lie like huge slugs among rusting oil drums.

36

the other, and that ended the scuffle. The loser flopped away backwards, and soon rolled over in sleep once more.

I stared out to sea, beyond the bay toward the distant Weddell Sea, Shackleton's implacable enemy. He had passed the mouth of this bay on his trip in the small boat, rowing against gigantic swells and headwinds, and made landfall in King Haakon Bay, a fjord just over the rocky headland on my left.

Above Shackleton, and now me, reared the snowy mountains which he and his companions had to cross to get help from the whaling station on Stromness Bay. When they showed up at the station, dirty with grease, raw with salt-water sores, haggard and in rags, they were not recognized as human beings.

The hard-bitten whalers wept to learn that this was indeed Shackleton, and to hear of the perils he had weathered. To them—and to me—Shackleton's experiences form the greatest epic in south polar exploration, the embodiment of courage and comradeship.

The cruise ship sounded the recall and interrupted my musings. Our last view of South Georgia was the bird islands at the western tip and the changeless snowy mountains.

Our course was now southwest toward the South Orkney group. These remote, high islands are notorious for bad weather and ice. They are usually blocked by bergs or pack ice from the Weddell Sea, and supply ships are often frustrated in their attempts to service the British weather station on Signy Island and the Argentine station on Laurie, the oldest meteorological station in the Antarctic, built by Scottish explorers.

The Orkney group was discovered in 1821 by sealing captains looking for new beaches to plunder. British George Powell met Yankee Nat Palmer at Elephant Island, and for safety in unknown seas, they went reconnoitering together. They found no seals, but Powell did find the South Orkneys for George IV of England.

We had learned by radio forecast that Signy Island was temporarily free of ice. From a distance, we saw the ice-crowned peaks of the islands glittering in the sunshine above a band of sea fog.

The British station on Signy was invisible behind a rocky ledge, except for cairn and radio mast. The station crew welcomed us—they hadn't seen a ship for months. "And you've brought us the first decent day in weeks," they said.

We surged ashore, and they showed us the laboratory facilities and outlined their various disciplines. Most

British artist-naturalist Keith Shackleton stands on the spot where his great-uncle made his first landfall after 4 months on an ice floe. He and his crew reached land at the east point of Elephant Island. The seals for which the island is named still loll on the narrow beach.

passengers made at once for the tiny room that served as post office. Antarctic stamps and cancellation marks were in great demand.

Our captain learned that he could skirt the pack ice by heading north. Our crunching, bumping progress through the pack had several times brought us to a shuddering standstill.

The change of course proved a bonanza. We would pass close to Elephant Island, the wild, bleak pyramid where Shackleton's party had landed and where 22 men survived 4½ winter months before being rescued.

In the distance, we saw the glistening peaks of a 3,000-foot mountain, and glaciers sloping direct to the sea. Closer, we perceived that small rock ledges were crowded with chinstrap penguins. Elephant Island is about 34 miles long and 3½ to 15 miles wide, and almost inaccessible. Our ship anchored off Cape Valentine, its pebbly beach strewn with the elephant seals for which the island is named.

One man on board, Keith Shackleton, was even more eager than I to reach the island. All his life he had heard heroic tales of his illustrious great-uncle, Sir Ernest Shackleton. How close we could get to the island depended on the captain's judgment.

He was generous. In the end, he allowed Keith, me and a friend to take an inflatable boat and search along the shore for Shackleton's two landing spots. We dressed warmly and belted on life jackets, though we would have lasted no more than a couple of minutes in the cold water.

Pinnacles are characteristic of the eastern end of Elephant Island. Cruise ship passengers followed in Shackleton's wake along the rugged shore past Cape Valentine, below, his first landfall.

With a spare motor, extra gas, generous lunches, a small flask of cognac and a portable radio, we pushed off. In exactly 6 hours we must be back aboard ship, or a rescue party would have to be sent out.

We ran close under the sheer cliffs, and at the eastern end of the island we spotted the gravel beach where Shackleton's three rowboats first landed. Debris falling from steep rock slides had made it too dangerous for them to remain. We found the slope still snow-covered, though it was now January, midsummer in Antarctica.

We followed in Shackleton's wake around the pinnacles that form the eastern end of the island and met heavy surf that deluged us with spray. The shore rose steeply, without foothold. In the mist we could scarcely see the penguins on ledges several hundred feet above us.

This was the most dismal setting I had ever seen, utterly forlorn and forbidding. What must it have been for those men with no shelter but a couple of upturned boats, hunger staring them in the face, and only the slimmest hope of rescue?

Ernest Shackleton left 22 men on this rugged beach on the north shore of Elephant Island while he went for help. Chinstrap penguins have created a long, curving road up and across the snowfield above the beach.

It was difficult for us to make any headway. Numb with cold, salt-encrusted and wet, we got an inkling of what Shackleton and his men went through. Keith skillfully guided our rubber boat, while keeping a sharp lookout for a niche that might have provided shelter for the castaways.

We knew that the storms of 60 years would have removed any trace of their encampment, but at least we hoped to identify the spot where 22 men survived the antarctic winter waiting for a chancy rescue.

We had to pass between a stranded iceberg and the shore, where the waves had undercut the berg and left it unbalanced. But Keith timed our speed accurately, and we passed through on a swell. We wondered if it was wise to continue, but we knew this opportunity would never come again. A nip of cognac revived our zeal and warmed our fingers and toes. Slowly Pinnacle Rock, an unmistakable landmark, appeared. We recognized it from old photographs. Our quest ended when we came to a break in the shoreline, the only possible refuge on shore, a snow-covered ledge where a heavy surf crashed on big rocks.

Above the ledge rose a snow slope, stained with the tracks of chinstrap penguins, their pathway between the

A sheathbill on a lichened ledge of Elephant Island's south shore looks down on red-jacketed tourists and a small group of chinstrap penguins on the rocks below. *Right*—The *Lindblad Explorer* waits offshore while passengers visit the chinstrap penguin colony. The tourists are in no danger of being overlooked among the birds, as has sometimes happened to stranded sailors.

nursery and the sea. Until they migrated north for the worst of the winter, chinstrap penguins had served as food and fuel for the 22 men on the beach.

There was no possibility of our landing. Our boat would have been overturned in a moment. But Keith turned off the motor, and we all experienced an eeriness of atmosphere—the ceaseless noise of the waves, the mysterious mist obscuring everything. Keith, not given to fancies, said later that he had felt The Presence which so often had guided his great-uncle, and which others had termed Sir Ernest's "uncanny intuition."

It had served him well in 1916. For after British, Uruguayan and Chilean attempts had failed, Sir Ernest begged to conduct a fourth try at rescue. Chile loaned him the little steamer *Yelcho,* steel hulled and thus not ideal for working in ice. "And this time Providence favored us," Shackleton recorded.

Under his personal command, the *Yelcho* had slipped past the ice pack and through the mist to snatch the men from imminent starvation. They had known The Boss would not fail them.

Reluctantly, Keith coaxed the motor into action again, and with the wind behind us, we each peeled an orange from our lunch. This commonplace action in that setting suddenly drove home to us the vast contrast between our comfortable voyaging and that of those brave, hardy men. The inner glow we experienced at having reached this grimly historic spot held us silent all the way back to the ship.   ◀◀◀

Elephant seals.

RICHARD HARRINGTON'S SECOND VOYAGE

South Pole ★

Antarctica

Ross Ice Shelf
McMurdo Sound

Indian
Ocean

Cape Adare Robertson Bay

Pacific Ocean

Macquarie Island

Campbell Island

Stewart Island

New
Zealand

Australia

0 500 1000 Miles

South from New Zealand: The Subantarctic Islands

South of the continents, a number of islands form stepping stones to the White Continent. Each is different, each a surprise of animal life and vegetation.

I always enjoy the changeover from temperate zones to polar scenes. It is particularly marked and rewarding when traveling south from New Zealand.

A friend and I had met at the airport of Invercargill on New Zealand's South Island. On a brilliant Sunday morning we rented a car and drove south through lovely pastoral country.

At Bluff, the southernmost town, we took a ferry to Oban, a summer resort on Stewart Island, the first of our stepping stones to the Antarctic. Its permanent residents are largely fishermen, and the old-fashioned hotels attract outdoor families on vacation.

Corriedale sheep graze near Bluff at the south tip of New Zealand's South Island.

The tiny resort village of Oban on Stewart Island is on the most southern tip of New Zealand. Scarlet-flowered rata trees and lush ferns are among the exotic vegetation of the island, an unspoiled nature preserve.

The proprietress herself showed us to our simple rooms and informed us that we could have our tea now in the lounge with the other guests.

They were all New Zealanders, none of whom had ever been to the Antarctic, but they were fairly well informed and contributed their information in friendly discussion. New Zealanders feel toward the Antarctic at their back door as Canadians feel about their Arctic. Not one in ten thousand goes there, but they are keenly aware of it and would like to see it for themselves. They spoke with enthusiasm of the various bird colonies on the subantarctic islands.

For a couple of days we strolled about the village and island. There is no paved road, indeed only 7 or 8 miles of gravel track, plenty for the few trucks on the island.

The village is a bower of greenery with immense trees, including a daisy tree I had never noticed elsewhere. We hiked over small paths through the rata forest, listening to a host of songbirds, including the bellbird, the tui and tomtits. On a quiet bay we spotted a blue penguin and a fat mollymawk. The water was too placid for the latter, which could not take off. But we saw not a single kiwi, though they are said to be more numerous here than anywhere else in the country.

44

The Auckland Islands shag forms a colony on Enderby Island. Nests are cupped mounds. *Below*—Though far south, Stewart Island boasts tall rata trees and is the home of the kiwi, the flightless bird that is the emblem of New Zealand.

Acclimatization societies were vigorous a century ago, setting out domestic and wild birds and animals with innocent zeal. They could not foresee the adverse effects these creatures might have on their new environment. Virginia deer and Australian opossum throve to the point where they are declared "noxious creatures," and a bounty is paid on them.

Pigs, cattle and rabbits were established on likely islands for the benefit of seamen and castaways. On still other islands settlement plans went astray, and domestic animals went bush. Cats preyed on flightless birds such as the kiwi, and rats have devastated ground-nesting species.

Having blundered so badly in the past, New Zealand now feels strongly about protecting the native flora and fauna. That is why some islands are closed to all visitors except a handful of scientists.

In our Zodiacs, the inflatable gray rubber boats, we cruised off the rocky steep-walled Snares Islands through kelp beds and looked longingly toward the magnificent chestnut-maned sea lions and fur seals on shore. The Snares are uninhabited now, since farming proved uneconomical, but wild cattle and pigs gone feral roam under the dense mat of wind-stunted rata forest.

An elephant seal
wallows in malodorous
puddles on Campbell
Island. *Below*—Long
tresses of seaweed
drip from the rock as the
tide runs out.

Large areas of the Auckland Islands are covered with tall rata forest and heath bushes.

Yellow-eyed penguins have a golden crown of feathers. The meteorological station on Campbell Island, New Zealand, registers rain on 322 days of the year.

We observed some royal albatrosses lumbering along a sandy beach, vainly trying to take off, but instead falling over for lack of wind lift. One cliff held a close-packed colony of shags, perched on built-up nests.

Farther south we came to Shoe Island, now uninhabited. A small cemetery told of farming tragedies and of seal hunters marooned here by their companions for revealing the locations of secret sealing beaches.

Here, for the first time, I encountered yellow-eyed penguins. They inspected us through brown-yellow eyes as curiously as we inspected them. This species is not gregarious like most penguins, preferring to live in small groups rather than in vast rookeries. Having by now seen half a dozen species, I was eager to see all 17. But only two men have accomplished that, one of them being fellow *Lindblad Explorer* passenger Roger Tory Peterson.

At Campbell Island, one of the Auckland group, we followed a winding channel to the neat meteorological station. Its small staff swells in summer with visiting scientists, but it gets few other visitors. When we arrived, the station crew had not yet gotten over its surprise at the casual visit yesterday of a Japanese fishing vessel. Two ships in just two days! They celebrated all over again.

Rarely can you expect a sunny day on remote Campbell Island, where the met station records rain on 322 days in the year. But we were lucky in a few hours of thin sunlight.

Campbell Island is noted as the home of the royal albatross, a beautiful bird with a wingspan reaching 11 feet, second in size only to its cousin the wandering albatross. The royal, too, mates only every second year to produce a single offspring. Rats have preyed on the nests, high-sided mounds of grass and mud.

A young zoologist studying this species led us up a steep path slippery with moisture to the windy summit slopes where the big birds nest. They perched on their high nests among the tussock grass, incubating the single egg. The proud birds allowed us close enough to see every fine feather in detail. The plumage of neck and head seemed the texture of ermine.

Campbell Island also has a history of abandoned farms, being too far off the shipping lanes. But 3,000 sheep are still there. It would have been too difficult and too costly to remove them, so the New Zealand government simply fenced them off on one end of the island. Scientists promptly seized upon the opportunity to measure the effect of grazing on the native cushion plant and ferns.

On the flatter ground near the station, elephant seals dozed in reeking wallows. Some mudholes were so deep I wondered how the creatures could ever get out, and the stalks of flowering bubunella seemed a bizarre touch. No

47

Clockwise—Bubunella (*Chrysobactron rossii*) is an uncommon plant of the Auckland Islands. Rough-leaved Macquarie cabbage grows profusely in gullies of Macquarie Island, the most southerly "green" island; the cabbage was popular with whalers and sealers. Macquarie's beaches are strewn with rocks and boulders, as well as slippery kelp washed up by the waves. On the horizon are The Nuggets, a local landmark.

one attempted to pick the coarse flowers, for the mud was very slippery. I hate to think what would happen if you slipped in the foul brown muck and found yourself sharing the bath with a 3-ton seal. What if you both tried to get out at the same time?

Elephant seals seem to have no racial memory of the slaughter of their species on Macquarie Island, or else they have forgiven mankind. This island was the scene of carnage until 1911, by which time the fur seals were exterminated. The island became a wildlife sanctuary in 1936, and gradually confidence has been restored.

Albatross fledglings ("big as turkey and tastier than pullet") are safe from hungry whalers. Elephant seals and penguins no longer fear the iron digesters rusting on shore. In fact, the seals sprawl over the station's fuel supply, and you can stumble over them when you step outdoors, if you're not careful.

Macquarie Island, the most southerly green island, sits on the edge of the Antarctic Convergence. I saw no bushes, but tussock grass flourishes, and so does the large round-leaved "cabbage"

so much appreciated by the scurvy-dreading sealers and whalers of the past.

With them gone, Macquarie Island is inhabited only by the cheerful, outgoing mob of Aussies at the Australian National Antarctic Research station, for this island comes under Australian administration.

Macquarie is known as the only homeland of royal penguins. Thirty-odd passengers braved the blustery cold wind and scrambled over the rough beach of upended stones to reach a rookery of royals, several thousand of them, massed together.

They look much like the macaronis and rockhoppers we had seen in the Falkland Islands, crested with topknots of yellow feathers. But the white feathers of the breast extend right up under the chin and even on to the cheeks.

This colony milled in two lines up and down a dry streambed, between their hungry chicks and the sea where their food was.

Practically oblivious to visitors, the outward-bound royal penguins gossiped constantly and excitedly about whatever

The Australian National Antarctic Research Expedition station was established on this stony isthmus of Macquarie Island in 1948. The waves rolling up on shore are polar waters of the Antarctic Convergence. Long strands of seaweed stream back and forth like long hair.

Adult royal penguins guard the nursery of downy young on Macquarie Island, the only place they breed.

penguins talk about. Those homeward bound couldn't say much with their beaks full of krill, the tiny shrimplike crustaceans that form the base of the food chain in Antarctica.

First the parent fills its own stomach, then loads up for the chick. Parents take turns on the nest and in the feeding. The turnaround may take days or even a week, but the two-way traffic seems to go on steadily in the nightless summer. Since you'll find royal penguins nowhere else, it's good to know that the several colonies total 2 to 3 million birds.

There was also a rookery of the big king penguins, another of gentoos with white ear patches, and small groups of rockhoppers. I wished I could stay a month on Macquarie.

But our next landfall was to be Cape Adare, due south of New Zealand on the White Continent itself.   ◄◄◄

49

Historic Antarctica

The Antarctic Continent has only a few historic sites, and they are relatively recent. By contrast to Europe, with its battlefields and evidences of several civilizations, in the Antarctic a little wooden hut represents history. It is hardly cluttered with these, and happily unscarred by war.

It was with considerable excitement that we drove through pack ice on a sunny January night and anchored off Cape Adare, the most northerly point of West Antarctica.

Clambering ashore at Robertson Bay, we found ourselves in a vast Adelie penguin colony which Sir James Clark Ross had described as "inconceivable myriads of penguins and an insupportable stench of guano." He named the bay for the surgeon of the *Terror,* the smaller of his two ships, and noted that it was backed by "perpendicular ice cliffs."

But Ross never landed on the continent itself, only took possession of it for his young Queen Victoria by raising the Union Jack on some small islands close to the mainland.

I walked with a friend along the edge of the rookery to three huts on the beach. Carstens Borchgrevink, having been the first man to set foot on the continent in 1895, returned in 1899 to be the first to winter on shore. He set up two prefabricated huts (one for storage and emergency). Unfortunately, he was not able to accomplish much because his party was trapped between unsafe sea ice and the towering wall of the Admiralty Range.

These huts, like another three south in McMurdo Sound, are historic sites, under the care of the New Zealand Antarctic Historical Society. Norris Baden, representing the society, accompanied us as guest lecturer. He

Mount Herschel rises clearly above other ice-clad peaks of the Admiralty Range on Victoria Land.

Left—The Borchgrevink party built this solid hut at Cape Adare in February 1899 and was the first group to winter successfully on the Antarctic Continent. The Adelie penguins are the most numerous penguin species; both sexes look alike. *Above*—The MacCormick skua, a predatory gull that feeds on penguin eggs and young.

had brought a bronze plaque printed in English, French, Spanish and Russian to be placed at the Borchgrevink hut.

No one had been here for several years, it seemed. We broke away ice from the solid door and entered the stuffy darkness of the windowless hut.

Inside were the original bunks, and even a small photographic darkroom with jars and bottles and trays.

"There's a special feeling in these historic huts," Mr. Baden said seriously. "It's as if the spirits of the Heroic Age were still present."

The third hut is neither as old nor as well built. It was put up hastily in 1911 by Scott's northern party, with only a couple of hammers, and the roof has fallen in.

There is no trace of a popular Finnish sauna that the two Lapp dog drivers built in a huge snowbank. They installed a small iron stove with a funnel poking up through the snow, and Borchgrevink's men reveled all winter in their steam bath.

Mr. Baden spent all his time ashore setting up his plaque and searching for the grave of the first man to die on the continent. He knew it was on a hillside but not which one. Eventually he located it, and the wooden cross had not crumbled in the dry antarctic air, though the lettering was indecipherable. It was a memorial to Nicolai Hanson, "one of the noblest and best of men." The biologist with Borchgrevink, dying of scurvy, asked to be buried here a thousand feet up the slope. A later expedition added his name to the grave, picked out in small stones.

We cruised south along the coast of Victoria Land, the Admiralty Range glistening to starboard. Mount Herschel, rising over 12,000 feet, was a landmark at Cape Hallett. Here a climbing party led by Sir Edmund Hillary found small quantities of gold and hematite in 1948.

Cape Hallett, a joint United States-New Zealand scientific station during International Geophysical Year 1957-58, may someday become a historic site. At present it is deserted and solidly locked up.

I walked among the various buildings and among the Adelie penguins that have reclaimed their ancestral breeding grounds. It was amusing to see how completely they had made themselves at home, having outwaited the human invaders.

We continued south into McMurdo Sound, where the floe ice we had been bucking merged into solid ice. This was the preferred route for many explorers since it is the debarcation point nearest to the South Pole. At the foot of the bay, McMurdo Base (U.S.) has grown to a large village, with an immense airstrip on the ice and complex installations befitting the largest base on the continent.

At Cape Hallett, Victoria Land, melting ice pans take fantastic shapes as they freeze and thaw in the November spring. In the background, the snowy Admiralty Range rises over 12,000 feet to pointed Mount Herschel. The cape was the site of a joint United States-New Zealand research station during the International Geophysical Year. The station, right, is now closed, and the Adelie penguins have regained their ancient nesting grounds.

Richard Harrington
at Cape Adare's Adelie
penguin rookery.

We did not visit McMurdo, though a U.S. Coast Guard icebreaker was carving a channel to it through the solid ice. Thoughtful American passengers wondered why the icebreaker carried cannon. "Do we need them? Isn't that against the Antarctic Treaty?" (Icebreakers are classed as warships and carry weapons; they are within the letter of the law.)

We returned to crunching through heavy brash ice and growlers the size of a house. Our ship vibrated as it struck ice, but the reinforced bow steadily broke a path through the floes, and I imagine our captain winced at every brutal encounter with the hard ice, like a car driver on a potholed road.

My cabin was at water level, and the porthole closed with an iron cover. But the ice pans sliding along the sides made a racket like a steel mill in full operation. I was sure the floor on which I stood buckled just a bit.

When I shaved in the morning, the lather on my face didn't foam properly, and the breakfast coffee tasted brackish.

"What's the matter?" I asked our Swedish waitress, who was looking troubled.

Well, the kitchen staff had just discovered that our water had a faintly salty flavor. Hitting a particularly tough ice pan, we had sprung a small leak in one fresh-water tank, which had now been closed off. It was mended a couple

A ship can always expect heavy pack ice in McMurdo Sound and must be built to break through it or push it aside.

of weeks later. "Only took a wad of chewing gum," the frogman claimed airily.

From a long way off, we sighted the magnificent landmark of Mount Erebus, rearing 12,450 feet high above the sound, a white plume streaming from its crater. Sometimes this volcano hurls rocks into the air as well as sulfurous gases. Next to it, both on Ross Island, is the extinct lower volcano, Mount Terror. Sir James named them for his two ships. He was not delighted to discover these mountains, for they barred him from his goal, the south magnetic pole.

Mount Erebus is the best known of numerous active volcanoes in Antarctica. That the frozen continent was once warm and supported a lush prehistoric vegetation is proved beyond doubt by seams of anthracite coal and fossilized tree trunks 17 feet long and 15 inches in diameter.

Was the climate tropical down here millions of years ago, or does this indicate that Antarctica once held a very different position among the land masses, proof that the continents have drifted wide apart?

Mounts Erebus and Terror stand over three historic cabins on Ross Island.

Shackleton's hut, the most northerly of the three, was built at Cape Royds in 1907. From here one group of his men climbed into the gassy crater of Mount Erebus and another group pinpointed the south magnetic pole, while he himself led a third party to within 97 miles of the South Pole.

Eight miles south is Scott's second hut at Cape Evans, from which he made his fatal trek to the South Pole late in 1911.

Another 12 miles south, on the edge of McMurdo Base, is Hut Point. The hut that was headquarters for Scott's explorations on the Ross Ice Shelf from

Shackleton's hut at Cape Royds was protected by low hills, and Pony Lake provided fresh water. On a snowy slope, three Adelie penguins toboggan on their bellies. A small sign has been set up asking visitors to respect the birds.

Clockwise—Shackleton's party was based here on the 1907-1909 expedition; the tablet proclaims it a historic site. One cache of provisions was located at a distance for emergencies; tins have scattered from the sprung cases. Bales of straw and boxes of provisions formed walls to stable four or five ponies.

1901 to 1903 still stands. The crew at Scott Station (N.Z.) 2 miles away acts as caretakers.

Our ship tied up to the ice at Cape Royds, and we surged ashore to spread out around the little meltwater pond and the penguin colony—the most southerly Adelies in the world. Compared with arctic latitudes, we were now at the equivalent of 400 miles north of Point Barrow, Alaska.

Shackleton and Scott both believed that hardy Mongolian ponies were superior to dogs for hauling sleds, so both their huts have improvised stables walled with bales of hay and straw. Oats lie in the packing-case mangers and bridles hang on the walls.

We walked on hallowed ground.

Inside the rehabilitated hut, we gazed in wonder at the utensils and clothing left behind in 1909. It didn't require much imagination to picture that gallant crew in these surroundings, and of course it meant even more to Keith Shackleton.

Shackleton's hut consists of
a single large room
and vestibule and a
very small photographic
darkroom. The shelves
hold tins of food,
even a wrapped ham. The
sleeping quarters, not
shown, contain equipment
left for the next expedition.

Outside the hut,
one dog kennel remains,
with bones preserved in
the arid atmosphere
since at least 1909.

57

With the captain's permission, three of us began walking across the ice along shore, and our steps naturally carried us south toward Scott's hut at Cape Evans. We stepped along briskly in the clean, cold atmosphere.

"No secondhand air for us!" exclaimed one of my companions. In the absolute clarity of atmosphere the cape seemed much closer than 8 miles. We walked single file, watchful of cracks where Weddell seals had crawled out to snooze in the sun.

Our ship grew smaller behind us as we trudged over the seemingly endless expanse of ice. We kept Barne Glacier on our left, and I calculated how quickly we might reach its comparative safety in case a strong wind came up and broke open our icy path.

Around a sweeping curve—the snout of the glacier—we lost sight of the ship, and now we felt totally alone in the immensity of ice. No sounds reached us. The sun shone, and we breathed deeply of the icy air.

Afar off we saw the object of our hike. Low and square, the prefabricated wooden building had been set up on the shore for ready transfer of stores from the ship. Again and again, the hut disappeared behind ice ridges and

Scott's hut at Cape Evans was used by Shackleton's "southern party" in 1915-16. Outside the hut, bales of hay and straw, grain and harness remain. Inside, everything remains in place. The hut holds a large coal stove, the large table, and in the rear, double-decker bunks.

58

A cairn and cross commemorate three men of the *Aurora,* Shackleton's southern party, who used Scott's hut. Outside the hut lie the mummified remains of one of Scott's dogs.

Scott's large prefabricated hut had an annex for travel gear and a shed for the ponies he used in his journey to the South Pole.

rocks on shore. Three hours after leaving the ship, we reached the two barricaded doors of the hut. Hearts thumping with excitement, we removed the barricades and entered.

We stepped into a spacious cabin fully equipped with food, cutlery, china. It looked as though the explorers had left yesterday, but the magazines and calendars bore the date 1911.

There were hundreds of tins of food— meat, fish, vegetables, sauces, rolls of pemmican, an unopened ham, tins of ship biscuits—both inside and out.

The food was not altogether identical to that left by the Scott expedition. Much of that had been used in 1915 to save the lives of a Shackleton party stranded at Cape Royds when their ship *Aurora* was swept out to sea. Shackleton punctiliously replaced every item later.

Undemocratically, to our minds, the cabin was divided by a white line into officers' and men's quarters. Then we remembered that this was previous to the 1914-18 war, when there was plenty of class distinction, and Scott was a captain in the Royal Navy. He believed the men preferred an area of their own, and certainly he needed privacy at times.

Scott and four companions, including the beloved Dr. Wilson ("Our Bill") left this hut late in 1911 on their world-famous expedition to the South Pole. They reached it successfully, but not first. Roald Amundsen had beaten them to it by a month.

Disappointed and in poor physical condition, Scott and his companions turned for home, but terrible gales held them windbound, and none of them returned to this hut at Cape Evans.

Three bodies, journals, letters and films were found a year later, only 11 miles from a food depot. The tent was reverently collapsed over the bodies to await burial at sea as the Ross Ice Shelf moved forward inexorably.

Outside Scott's hut, we stood on Lookout Hill, a knoll with a cross on it. From this little hill, Scott's men had watched for his return, and later for the relief ship. The cross was not for Scott, however, but for three men of the *Aurora* who had survived starvation and scurvy only to plunge through thin ice.

We borrowed a china cup from the cabin to drink from the glacier runoff outside, feeling like intruders. Near the little stream I found a food dump, 200 yards from the hut. Supplies had been cached there presumably in case of fire, that menace of men wintering on the ice. But sadly I noticed that all the tins had recently been opened by ax or some other sharp tool to reveal 60-year-old ship biscuits. Some were spoilt by meltwater.

I tried one, and it was no worse than ship biscuits usually are. But with moisture in the tins, they would not last another 60 years, even in arid, bacteria-free Antarctica.

We pondered in silence in that vast frozen landscape before we replaced the barricades at the doors and hurried back to our ship. Passengers lined one rail, cheering our returning footsteps. We were almost ashamed to travel in luxury

59

Clockwise—During the brief antarctic summer, two students of Canterbury University, New Zealand, study glacial meltwater for its chemical components. This small hut at Cape Bird, Ross Island, is used by the New Zealand study teams. The New Zealand personnel at Scott Station still use sled dogs for a good deal of transportation.

where the explorers strove against such odds.

We realized, too, that we had been lucky. Even that short hike had involved some hazard. A whirling blizzard could have sprung up without warning, obliterating landmarks, or the ice could have split, opening impassable cracks. We felt exhilarated to have shared some of the perils the explorers knew.

On the eastward end of Ross Island there is a notable rookery of emperor penguins, the largest of their species. For a long time, explorers believed that this was their only nursery on the continent, but many more have been found.

We hoped against hope that some might still be there.

In vain, for this penguin breeds only in winter, on the ice. The female lays a single egg, then goes off to sea to feed up after a long fast. The males gather in groups, each one incubating an egg on his black feet. When the chick hatches, the mother returns and both parents fish constantly to still the hungry squawks of the fast-growing fledgling.

Icebergs in the Antarctic are usually tabular to begin with, having broken from an ice shelf. This ice island is pierced by several wave-eroded tunnels.

Since the emperor reaches 48 inches in height, the chick must be well launched before another winter's blizzards. When the ice breaks up in spring the chick is ready to migrate northward for the summer.

Beyond Ross Island stretches the Ross Ice Shelf. "As well try to sail through the cliffs of Dover," Ross noted sadly, abandoning his hope of reaching the south magnetic pole by water.

The shelf ice is created by glaciers pushing down from Antarctica's mountainous interior. The weight forces the ice seaward at the rate of 4 feet a day. The extruded ice rests on the water, a floating shelf. Eventually the edge breaks and new flat-topped icebergs are born.

Thus nothing remains of the Bay of Whales, where Amundsen moored the *Fram* while he hiked off to achieve the South Pole ahead of Scott.

Nothing remains of five Little Americas set up by Richard E. Byrd; all have been carried into the sea.

There is no notch in the barrier ice to mark the spot where Scott and then Shackleton made a balloon ascent in 1901 to peer over the wall of ice. They saw only more ice, an apparently endless vista, which extended halfway to the pole, as they later discovered on foot.

We skirted this icy wall, which varies in height from 15 to 600 feet and extends over an area as large as France. We felt its icy breath. I saw fierce winds rip along its face, whirling clouds of icy particles seaward.

Unlike the early navigators who had to rely on sail and skill to get through the ice pack, our captain had a current satellite map to show him the extent of ice off the coastline.

We swung northward in Bellingshausen Sea, away from the great bulge of Marie Byrd Land, and in the distance spotted Peter I Island.

Antarctic travel hinges on weather conditions and the position of the pack ice. I've been lucky on three voyages to make unexpected landfalls, but Peter I Island remained inaccessible.

Bellingshausen named it for his emperor, Peter the Great, but he got no closer to it than we did.

In 1929, a group of Norwegians landed on the high island, the only ones ever to step ashore on this isolated mound of rock and snow. It is said to hold a small hut that the Norwegians set up and stocked with emergency supplies.

They may still be there, for the island is always surrounded by miles of pack ice. We passed 25 to 30 miles to the north, for the captain had no taste for risking his ship in the pack ice that lay between us. Keith Shackleton and Roger Tory Peterson looked at the island with hungry eyes. No one has ever done a bird count on Peter I.

We soon approached the islands off the Antarctic Peninsula, the Antarctic's most dramatic scenery.

Since I approached it from the north, from Tierra del Fuego, it might be as well to start there. ◄◄◄

On McMurdo Sound, a plaque on the Scott hut commemorates the British Antarctic Expedition. The icy mountains of Victoria Land flank the sound where the surrounding snowfields and Mount Lister are colored pastel by the low sun.

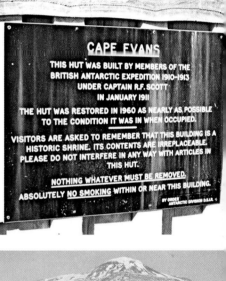

Iceberg, 200 to 300 feet high.

RICHARD HARRINGTON'S THIRD VOYAGE

Atlantic Ocean

South
America

●Ushuaia

Deception Island

Antarctic Peninsula

Tierra del Fuego

Antarctica

Pacific Ocean

★
South Pole

|0 |500 |1000 Miles

The Antarctic Peninsula

Way down at the tip of South America is the archipelago of Tierra del Fuego, named the Land of Fire by Magellan when in 1520 he saw the campfires of the Ona and Yaghan aborigines.

On the southern rim of the largest island is Ushuaia, the most southerly town in the world. It is a seaport, and the terminus of the Pan American Highway, 8,000 miles from its beginning in Alaska.

During the Christmas holidays, Argentines escape the midsummer heat of Buenos Aires by driving 2,000 miles down the highway to cooler latitudes where the snow-capped Andes slip beneath the sea to reappear as islands and the icy ranges of the Antarctic Peninsula.

Tourists camp beside Lakes Roca and Fagnano in the Parque Nacional de Tierra del Fuego, near Ushuaia. Here the flora is already subantarctic,

Adelie penguins follow the leader across a thin ice bridge beside Hope Bay at the tip of the Antarctic Peninsula.

The most southerly town in the world is Ushuaia, population about 4,000. Ships supply Argentine bases in Antarctica from here each summer, November to February. They must cross dreaded Drake Passage, rarely as calm as in the bottom photo.

Once labeled "the uttermost part of the earth," Estancia Harberton, a sheep station in southern Tierra del Fuego, displays a colorful garden of lupines and orange lilies, despite the rugged, windy climate.

comprising forests of antarctic beech and wild fuschia.

Estancia Harberton, fronting on Beagle Channel, is the most southerly sheep ranch in the world. Here Lucas Bridges wrote the classic book of white settlement on Tierra del Fuego, appropriately titled *The Uttermost Part of the Earth.*

When I visited Bridges' relatives, the Goodall family (Mrs. Natalie Goodall had been an Ohio schoolteacher), they showed me first their lush garden of flowers and vegetables, then their outdoor museum, including a whale skeleton. The two small daughters collected shells and played happily on their swing, unconcerned that 50 air miles separated them from school playmates in Ushuaia.

On my first visit to Tierra del Fuego 20 years ago, I cruised from Ushuaia to

Navarino Island south of Beagle Channel and met the last surviving Yaghan Indian, a desiccated crone named Yulia, who had outlived not only her family but her entire race.

And I ventured farther south to the Cape Horn Islands, looked across the water toward the Antarctic Continent, and yearned to go farther.

Ushuaia, then a sleepy, easygoing naval base, is now crowded with oil seekers who believe there are great quantities of oil out in Drake Passage, the 570-mile-wide strait between Tierra del Fuego and the Antarctic Peninsula. The waters of Pasaje de Drake are believed the world's stormiest, so that the sea floor is littered with wrecked ships. But on three occasions I have seen the rugged cape in calm weather, once so serene that our ship glided within a mile of the cliffs. We saw sheep on summer pasture and could study every cranny filled with nesting sea birds.

Yet on another occasion when crossing the Antarctic Convergence in Drake Passage, the turbulence made us strap ourselves into our berths.

For eventually I got my wish to visit the Antarctic, leaving from Ushuaia and crossing Drake Passage to cruise along the Antarctic Peninsula.

Swedish-American Lars-Eric Lindblad was the first to envision tourists in Antarctica. In 1969, he chartered a ship to carry passengers in style to the fringe of the frozen continent. To enhance their understanding and enjoyment, he invited as guest lecturers experts in history and natural sciences.

Snow falls even in summer in Tierra del Fuego's subantarctic climate, making these beeches look like a Chinese landscape painting.

Yulia, last surviving Yaghan Indian, over 80.

The *Lindblad Explorer* is surrounded by floating ice at Port Lockroy, Anvers Island.

Lars-Eric Lindblad of New York, innovator of the Antarctic tourist cruises, tells a passenger about the lives of the chinstrap penguins at their feet.

On the ship by which I traveled three times to the Antarctic, the *Lindblad Explorer,* there was a real thirst for information. We learned a lot from the experts aboard, in lectures and private conversations, and conned books in the ship's specialized library for detailed information or to settle an argument.

The Lindblad cruises have proved successful to the point of emulation. An Argentine vessel now makes several cruises during the southern summer, carrying about 600 passengers each time. This is not entirely to build up a tourist business, but to involve Argentines emotionally in their country's territorial claim to "Argentina del Sur."

But tourists reached Antarctica decades ago. The first woman visitor was the wife of a Norwegian whaling captain in 1935. Then came the wife of famous whaler Lars Christensen, with three friends. Their visit is commemorated by Four Ladies Bank, off Queen Maud Land.

The only women, so far, to winter on the continent are two Americans. Mrs. Finn Ronne and Mrs. Harry Darlington meant only to see their husbands well launched on the Ronne expedition of 1947-48, the last private antarctic expedition. Instead they found themselves "beset by ice" and unable to leave.

A ring of pack ice girdles the continent south of the convergence, its position varying according to wind and currents. It took explorers in wooden sailing ships a week or twice that to break through to open water closer to land.

The White Continent had sent us tokens of its presence in the form of icebergs. Some tabular bergs broken from shelf ice have measured 5,000 square miles, the size of Connecticut. "Ice islands," the explorers called them, correctly.

Others were in fantastic shapes, fluted and tunneled, sculpted by wind and wave. (Some people have suggested towing huge bergs northward across the equator to thirsty California.)

When the first iceberg was announced from the bridge, the dining room emptied in 20 seconds. We saw a white pimple in the distance, but cameras began to click and whir at once.

"Hold your fire," repeaters advised the newcomers. "Wait until we start nosing right among the bergs."

A grounded iceberg displays beautifully fluted sides, the design created by wave action. A dominican gull perches on top.

Solid and placid as they look, the icebergs are dangerous, and not only because eight-ninths are under water, but because the sea constantly erodes them. Their point of gravity changes and then the bergs slowly topple over to find a new balance. The tunnels and arches and undercuts have a further danger, because a surge from an overturning berg could suddenly fill them with water and crush us and our frail inflatables against the roof.

An arch in a tabular berg makes a frame for a boatful of tourists.

67

The small iceberg above, the size of a two-story house, is called a growler. An archway in a much larger berg is explored by tourists in inflatable rubber boats.

Keith Shackleton, Roger and Barbara Peterson and I once got permission to cruise among the bergs for photographs, promising to take every caution. We crept under a couple of arches and glided through an ice tunnel, water dripping down our necks. We saw a leopard seal yawning on an ice pan, and penguins standing statue-like on a berg like a modernistic stage. But half an hour later, our hearts skipped a beat, for the scenery had shifted completely. The berg had already overturned.

Excitement increased as we penetrated the ring of pack ice and the far-off ice-clad mountains showed luminous on the skyline. We stared in unbelief at the glistening mountains of the Antarctic Peninsula. A golden light kept passengers on deck until after midnight.

The abundant wildlife—both birds and beasts—along the shore of the Antarctic Peninsula and its fringing islands is a major attraction to tourists.

Four species of penguins breed on the peninsula—Adelie; chinstrap, with a thin line of black feathers across its white throat; the timid, slightly larger gentoo, with white patches above each eye; and the emperor, rarely found north of Marguerite Bay, our last port of call.

The Antarctic Peninsula thrusts northward from the continent of Antarctica like a finger crooked toward Tierra del Fuego. It is a mountainous spine, in places only 25 miles wide. Its steep shores rise to glacier-draped heights of 13,750 feet in the Eternity Mountains of Palmer Land.

It is a much-named, much-claimed peninsula. The Americans named it Palmer Peninsula after the sealer Nat Palmer, who believed himself first to see the mainland. Chile calls it Tierra O'Higgins, while Argentina resolutely

Left—A surrealistic iceberg forms a stage for a group of migrating Adelie penguins. They are catching a ride back to their ancestral breeding grounds.

Above—Chinstrap penguins sit on nests of small stones near a wooden cross at the deserted Chilean Gonzales Videla Station. Bare, rocky beaches, which most penguins need for nesting, are in short supply in Antarctica. *Left*—A rosy glow mantles mountain and snowfield on the Antarctic Peninsula, where every hour of the long summer day and night brings new colors.

69

Above—Port Lockroy on Anvers Island in the Palmer Archipelago was an important shore station for whalers before it became a British research station. It is now deserted. *Above right*—Huge glaciers coming off the high plateau of the Antarctic Peninsula eventually break off into the sea. *Right*—Constant wave action undermines the iceberg. When it becomes unbalanced, it will overturn.

labels it Tierra San Martin. These claims overlap one another, and the British claim the peninsula as Graham Land.

By the Antarctic Treaty which grew out of the remarkable accord of International Geophysical Year, the crooking finger is now firmly labeled Antarctic Peninsula. Graham Land is merely the slender northern segment, and Palmer Land the thicker base of a peninsula 600 or 900 miles long depending on where you measure from.

By the Antarctic Treaty, all territorial claims were frozen for 30 years, until 1991. Other main principles of the treaty were the use of the land for peaceful purposes only; international scientific cooperation; preservation and conservation of living resources.

Antarctica is the highest, coldest and least known of the continents. The South Pole perches at 10,000 feet, compared with the North Pole at sea level. The average land level is 6,000 feet, but half of that is ice. Antarctica can claim 80% of the world's ice, though only 10% of the earth's surface. If all that ice were to melt, the sea level would rise by hundreds of feet, drowning seaports and flooding lowlands around the world. At the same time, the land, relieved of its burden of ice, would rise even higher than before.

Left—A gentoo penguin has raised two chicks on a wooden box left behind at Port Lockroy. Below—A rare all-black Adelie nests on Weincke Island in the Palmer Archipelago.

Emergency shelter at Potter Cove, King George Island in the South Shetlands. Visitors are warned not to step on the centuries-old moss.

And of course the climate would moderate. At present the average annual temperature around the coast is zero Fahrenheit. The lowest temperature was recorded at Vostok, an inland meteorological station of the USSR, as -127° F. That's cold! Add a wind and it's perishing.

The winds make the country hostile to man, much more so than in the Arctic. Winds have been clocked up to 200 miles an hour and 80-mile gales can blow for 2 days without letup.

Scientists at stations on the Antarctic Peninsula and the nearby islands consider themselves in the banana belt. Temperatures average a cozy 26° F here, whereas the average at South Pole Station (U.S.) is -60° F. Precipitation in the Palmer Archipelago runs to 23 inches a year, compared with less than 2 inches at the pole.

Penguins are the trademark of Antarctica as wildlife is the hallmark of all Lindblad cruises. Tourists find the penguins irresistible, so cute, so

71

accessible and so fearless. We encountered as many at Hope Bay on the tip of the Antarctic Peninsula as at Cape Adare, on the western tip of the continent.

In the water, the leopard seal makes many a good meal out of a penguin. Several times I have seen the predator snatch a swimming bird and shake it out of its skin before devouring the body. This seal will even rock a small ice pan on which a penguin sits, so that the bird will slide off into its wide mouth.

It is a curious sight to watch a horde of Adelie penguins line up on shore, peering down into the water to see if a leopard seal is patroling. Somehow— does it fall or is it pushed?—one penguin plunges in. If it proves safe, the others follow with a tumult of splashing.

Even more fascinating is to watch the return. A sloping beach is very nice, but I have seen them leap straight up onto a rock ledge or ice shelf fully 7 feet above the water. It's so sudden, like the cork out of a champagne bottle, that the camera can scarcely catch the action.

Beaches along Bransfield Strait are again crowded with several species of seals, including the elephant and the gray Weddell. The fur seals once so thick it was impossible to walk among them almost vanished under the sealers'

The several million Adelies at Hope Bay have one line of traffic into the water and another returning to the nests. Those entering study the water cautiously for a leopard seal; if nothing happens to the first one in, the others follow.

An Adelie penguin leaps out of the water toward an ice shelf 6 to 8 feet above, but falls back in, to the apparent concern of those crowding the edge of the shelf on Hope Bay.

clubs. Happily, the population is building again under strict protection.

Wherever we landed, we used the buddy system, not for fear of animal attack, but because the rough beaches could easily result in tripping or slipping.

In another sensible safeguard, we were all issued scarlet parkas for ready visibility. More than once, shipwrecked sailors waving frantically to a rescue ship have been mistaken for penguins, and been overlooked. (We dubbed ourselves a new species, *Penguinnus lindbladios,* red-coated, red-headed, red-faced.)

I lay on the stones in this rookery, camera angled upwards. The ground was red and reeking with krill slopped over in regurgitating it into the mouths of the young, and the stench of droppings was almost overpowering. A portly little Adelie waddled toward me and dropped a pebble under my nose—an invitation to set up housekeeping!

I never expected to be propositioned by a penguin.

A long Weddell seal seems annoyed at being disturbed on its ice pan.

In the spectacular scenery of Hope Bay, a tourist sits on a rock to observe the Adelie penguins.

Hope Bay's Adelies have few enemies. One is the skua, above. A newer one is the husky, which it will walk past fearlessly. Often only a red stain on the snow remains.

Much as we were amused by penguin behavior, it is serious business to them. They have occupied the same nesting areas for thousands of years, returning to home base faithfully after a northern vacation. It's hard to resist attributing human behavior to them, and feeling sorry for the death of even a weak chick.

On shore, the only natural enemy is the skua, which nests right in the rookery where it can steal unprotected eggs or even a young bird. They are fierce in defending their own young. More than once I have been painfully clipped by a skua's wing tip. It makes you nervous when this big gull dive-bombs you in great swift loops. I took to wearing a thick woolen cap.

They even hovered a yard above me, talons outstretched, shrieking defiance. Any invader retreats from an outraged skua defending its hidden nest.

Astonishingly, a skua was sighted 200 miles from the South Pole by the Scott expedition, who marveled at what the bird lived on, so far from any food source.

The penguins of Hope Bay have acquired another enemy on land, the tethered huskies of Esperanza Station (Argentine).

The sled dogs are staked out across a slope above the sea, a route the Adelies have followed for generations. They have no racial memory that makes them fear dogs, so they waddle right up to the chained huskies. Often all that's left is a red stain on the snow.

Though many of the scientific stations put up during International Geo-

physical Year have served their purpose and are now closed, eight nations still maintain posts on the continent and the islands. We visited those of six nations. Most have small crews, up to a dozen men, though McMurdo Base (U.S.) has many more. The total population of Antarctica varies from possibly 400 in winter to four times that in summer.

The coast offers few suitable building sites, even if you expropriate penguin ancestral nesting grounds. Usually the stations are built on tiny rock promontories and are crowded by glaciers. At Almirante Brown (Argentine) you feel you'll be pushed into Paradise Bay any minute. At Palmer Station (U.S.) a lot of blasting was needed to create a reasonably flat area of 2 to 3 acres. Palmer is further confined by an ever-growing dump, everything in it well preserved in the dry atmosphere.

Garbage disposal is even more of a problem in the Antarctic than in our big cities. You can't bury it. Incinerate it and you pollute the atmosphere, to the horror of meteorologists. Tow it out to sea and you scandalize the oceanologists. Return it to the country of origin? Who wants it? Besides, it costs too much.

Upper left—Antarctic stations have a serious garbage disposal problem. Argentine station Esperanza burns what it can, but burial of the remainder is impossible in solid rock. *Left and below*—The snug buildings of Argentina's Almirante Brown sit on a narrow rock ledge between glaciers and Paradise Bay. Its dozen men welcome rare visitors.

Each of the stations seemed a microcosm of its homeland. Perhaps isolation strengthened and crystallized national characteristics.

The Antarctic leaves an indelible impression on all who spend time there. Most appear to love it. I am familiar with the signs of cabin fever from living in the Canadian Arctic, but I saw only one or two instances of men withdrawn and uncommunicative.

All nationalities, without exception, wanted to talk. Usually the station personnel were invited aboard ship, an exchange of hospitality for allowing us to swarm through their buildings and ask innumerable questions. They were delighted with the opportunity to tuck into fine food and drink. On occasion, some had to be helped gently into the last boat going ashore. They particularly enjoyed chatting with our pretty Swedish maids, but were sometimes awkwardly trapped by question-filled graybeards.

The New Zealanders from Scott Station in McMurdo Sound struck me as exceptionally cheerful, adaptable and able, much like their countryman Sir Edmund Hillary.

Obviously glorying in outdoor life and thriving on it, they use their excellent

U.S. Palmer Station on Anvers Island is exceptionally comfortable by antarctic standards, but it may eventually be overwhelmed by its enormous growing garbage dump. There is still pristine beauty nearby, such as this nunatak, right, which is a rock poking through an ice field.

76

dog teams for long journeys of exploration and study. Even when they pitch their tents on sea ice, they find time for a friendly cup of tea.

Many scientists, especially at the American stations, come only for a couple of summer months, with only a skeleton crew in winter.

Men sign on for 2 years in the British Antarctic Survey, and I met some who were doing a second, even third tour of duty, despite the low pay. They seemed to regard it as adventure.

As far as I know, no women have ever wintered at any of the stations, though a few get there in summer, including the USSR interior stations. I met a couple of young women from New Zealand studying solar force and penguins on Ross Island.

The Americans have by far the most comfortable stations, almost luxurious with wall-to-wall carpeted lounge and numerous pinups everywhere. All were eager to explain their subjects of research, often so esoteric I could not follow.

These men had dived into the ocean and retrieved fish that seemed equipped with antifreeze instead of blood, so that they could live happily in water a degree or so below freezing.

There were sea slugs and sea urchins. We saw sponges more than a foot across, 10-legged sea spiders half that size, starfish half as large again and a century old.

Australians were very open, much at ease, and given to hearty laughter. They at once offered beer, then proceeded in rapid speech to talk of their ex-

Left top—Whale bones bleach on the rocks at Port Lockroy. Beyond, gentoo penguins come to breed.
Bottom—U.S. Antarctic Research ship *Hero* approaches Palmer Station.

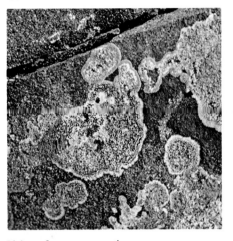

Lichens form on antarctic rocks like surrealistic paintings.

periences. All of them claimed to enjoy their stay in the Antarctic, but added, "You people moving around the edge of the continent see more in 3 weeks than we do in a 2-year stint."

Men at the Argentine and Chilean stations greeted us with loud tango music pouring from loudspeakers attached to their buildings. They were expansive, eyes flashing, and insisted that we see every last cubbyhole. They fed us strong black coffee and freshly made bread. They played the piano and sang lovely Latin American songs.

On King George Island in the South Shetlands we were surprised to find a Chilean station only a few yards from a Soviet station. Animated tangos blasted through the chill air in competition with Russian folksongs.

Bellingshausen (USSR) had at least two buildings adorned with humorous cartoon murals. Yet the big burly men just sat and glowered, until a New Yorker among us passengers spoke to them in fluent Russian. Then their eyes lit up. Shoulder-slapping began. Photos? Of course. Where do you want me to stand? They offered us borscht and black bread.

They all crowded around our interpreter, who could scarcely satisfy their curiosity. So much for snap impressions!

And now we learned why the dissimilar stations were so close together. The Chileans had been located on Deception Island until it erupted, wrecking their station. The Russians had shared their own patch of relatively flat space.

78

A glacier looms over an abandoned Chilean station, Gonzales Videla, in Paradise Bay. Its men had built a shrine to the Virgin Mary; a gentoo penguin now nests there. At King George Island, the Soviet Bellingshausen Station at far right shares its ground with the brown buildings of the Chilean Eduardo Frei Station.

Landings can be extremely hazardous at the remote British Antarctic Survey station on Adelaide Island, due to shifting pack ice. The cruise ship patrols rather than anchor, and the visit lasts less than an hour. Luckier hosts are at the B.A.S. station below, in the Argentine Islands. It has a sunny window for a small greenhouse and is painted black to trap any heat from the sun.

Back on ship, we were delighted to learn that Deception Island was our next port of call. But we bypassed it because of a storm that made it dangerous to attempt the narrow passage, and went farther south through a tangle of islands and channels, magnificent scenery. We hoped to land at Deception on our return north.

I particularly enjoyed our visit to the British Antarctic Survey station on the Argentine Islands. The crew of eight sat in their shirt sleeves on rocks in the sunshine, and welcomed our arrival with cheers. Some had luxurious bushy beards.

As at other B.A.S. stations they lived simply but had a fine cozy bar. They understated their achievements—all except the growth of plum-size green tomatoes they had grown in a windowed section. One man doted on their single pet husky dog.

The following day, we crossed the Antarctic Circle in water that was almost free of floating ice. Passengers crossing for the first time received a certificate from the captain.

About 100 miles farther south, we made our last call at a B.A.S. station on the southern edge of mountainous Adelaide Island, at Marguerite Bay, which is notorious for pack ice and fast ice.

No cruise ship had ever called there, and supply vessels occasionally had to miss a year. But we were invited over the ship's radio, and the crew of eight men had scoured and housecleaned in anticipation. They had seen no one but themselves for nearly a year and were eagerly looking forward to our visit—particularly to seeing the women. None had ever darkened their doors until now. They looked forward to dinner on board, a few drinks and conversation.

They showed us their lounge with its library and small bar, almost depleted now, but the supply ship was expected soon.

They were eager for any reading material—newspapers, paperbacks, even the ship's menus. And I recalled that a copy of a girlie magazine had been enthusiastically traded at the Soviet station for some canceled stamps and shoulder badges.

We hadn't been ashore an hour before we were summoned back to the ship. The pack ice was moving in. Only with the greatest difficulty were the passengers loaded into the rubber boats and returned to the ship.

Two hundred yards of moving ice had dashed the station crew's dream of a memorable social event. However, by pushing the boats over the ice pans, our Swedish seamen managed to take some treats ashore to the lonely men. ◀◀◀

Tourists at left are landing on the cinder beach of steaming, volcanic Deception Island, and climbing at far left to its inner rim, where the ground is still hot. A few hardy souls even brave the water, below, warm only at the surface.

Deception Island

Chinstrap penguin.

Fire and Ice! There is always a piquancy about finding them in the same place, whether in Alaska or Antarctica. In the latter, numerous volcanic islands still hurl smoke and ashes into the freezing polar air.

Mount Erebus on Ross Island looming over McMurdo Sound is the best-known volcano, but there are several in the South Sandwich Islands, visited only by research vessels.

The most dramatic and storied volcanic island is Deception, far south in the South Shetland group, and completely unlike other islands in the group.

When you first see it, the island appears to be only a steep-sided mound of rock with an unusually small amount of snow. But appearances are deceptive. It is actually a broken ring. You can't see the opening until you are squarely in front of it.

Then you sail through the narrow passage called Neptune's Bellows and find yourself in a salt-water pond 9 miles across, called Port Foster.

The harbor is actually the breached crater of a lively volcano. Ever since its discovery in 1820, Deception's sheltered water has been a haven from the storms that scour the strait between the South Shetlands and the Antarctic Peninsula.

From here on a clear day you can see the continent easily. But the early explorers, sealers and whalers who used the harbor as a rendezvous obviously didn't get many clear days.

81

Below—A twisted mass of girders and broken walls is all that remains of the Chilean weather station on Deception Island.
Right—Part of a whale's vertebra lies on the island's cinder beaches, and chinstrap penguins stand amid forgotten whaling machinery at its harbor.

Through the centuries, the volcano has blown its stack at irregular intervals. The most recent eruptions began a series in 1967, and the ground has not cooled off yet.

In that eruption, both Chilean and British meteorological stations were destroyed. Only twisted girders and a tangled mass of gear remain.

We landed in a heavy vapor rising at the water's edge. Some passengers worried that the seams of our rubber boats might come unstuck in the hot water. But it wasn't that hot, only about the temperature of a hot bath.

In fact, two or three high-spirited passengers, including an indomitable Australian woman, went for a swim. They found the water too hot for comfort at the surface, but very cold only a foot below. Their lips turned blue and their teeth chattered before they got into dry clothing. But they had set a record few of their friends could challenge—bathing in the Antarctic.

There are many interesting things along the beach. Old whaleboats filled with cinders, either washed there or engulfed by the rain of ashes. Bleached white whale vertebrae lying about, wooden hogsheads once meant to carry home whale oil, now lying with staves sprung.

Whaling was carried on from Deception Island for about 10 years, when the technique changed in the early 1920's and shore stations were outmoded.

The station has folded in upon itself, the great stacks askew with the recent eruptions. But in 1926, the great warehouse served as a hangar for Sir Hubert Wilkins' pioneer aircraft. This vigorous Australian-American saw that airplanes were the key to antarctic discovery and was the first to fly in Antarctica.

He took off from the small landing strip I saw beside the water. He had counted on a thick bed of snow to form a runway, but the island's warmth spoiled the plan. He had to set to work and scoop and shovel stones to create his landing strip. Though it was dangerously short, he managed to fly over the islands fringing the Antarctic Peninsula before he and Lincoln Ellsworth made their historic flights over the mainland.

As I walked along the beach in a clammy warm mist, suddenly a chinstrap penguin eased out of the water and waddled up the beach, its stubby red feet bleached pink from the hot water. It looked lonely and bewildered.

Oddly enough, the huge colony of chinstraps had known about the coming eruption of 1967 before the meteorologists suspected it. Two days before the blast, every last penguin abandoned its nest and chicks or eggs, and took off to sea.

Now here was one returned to its ancient nesting ground. Evidently I was a disappointment and did not

compensate for the lack of its peers, for it slid back into the water and swam away.

We took an uphill hike over snowy slopes and in half an hour reached the site of the most recent eruption. The heat of the lava could be felt through our boot soles. Steam hissed from many fumaroles, and bubbling sounds rose from the depths of crevices.

I visited Deception Island again briefly a year later. We had time only for a walk of an hour or so across the island on the other side of Port Foster, to a saddle overlooking the sea.

We looked down, and there below us, to our delight we saw a huge colony of chinstraps had reestablished themselves. The penguins rode in on big waves, landed on rock ledges in a heavy spray—and were frequently washed off again. They shook their stocky bodies, then lunged up the cliff to spell off their incubating mates. I hope my lonesome friend was among them. ◀◀◀

Wooden barrels, once intended for shipping whale oil, are sprung and useless now. The squared gap in the rocky ring is the entrance to Deception Island's harbor, Neptune's Bellows.

83

Birds and Mammals of the Antarctic

The Antarctic's abundant animal life lives in close association with the icy sea. From left are a Weddell seal at its breathing hole, an unusually light-colored young crabeater seal blending into the snow chunks, and a fearless, intelligent leopard seal, whose main diet is penguin flesh.

Elephant seals in typical poses, clockwise from right. The faces of the pups have a variety of expressions, generally appealing, but invariably the eyes, nose and mouth drip. Young seals spend most of their time sleeping on the beach, waiting to complete their molt. Dimwitted on shore, they are alert at sea as adults. Molting young seals about 10 feet in length indulge in small battles that are really a test of ramming power. At maturity they can measure 20 feet and weigh 4 tons.

Left top— A watchful male fur seal. *Bottom*—Kerguelen fur seals like the tussock grass of South Georgia and will snap at an invader, even bite, but they are easily driven back with a small stick. *Below*—A harem-master sea lion at the tip of Argentina nudges a female on the rocky ledges he guards vigilantly from rivals.

The 25-inch-tall rockhopper penguin is recognized by its yellow feather eyebrows above red eyes, giving it a deceptively sinister look. Penguins characterize the Antarctic. Only 4 of the 17 species actually breed on the continent itself. The rockhopper colony above is on New Island, being photographed by ornithologist Roger Tory Peterson. As the name implies, they jump from rock to rock.

An adult chinstrap penguin sits beside its large chick. It is readily identified by the narrow black facial line and feeds on krill.

Chinstraps have formed a colony on the south shore of Elephant Island. There is ceaseless movement among them, some heading for the water, some away from it, some waddling, others tobogganing.

The gentoo penguin, 30 inches tall, has a triangular white patch above the eye. It breeds on the Antarctic Peninsula but is more widespread on the subantarctic islands. It eats krill rather than fish.

Usually only one gentoo chick survives, but here twins poke their beaks into a parent's mouth to be fed regurgitated krill.

A colony of several thousand king penguins have settled amid the tussock grass at the Bay of Isles, South Georgia. The downy chick at left little resembles its magnificent, 3-foot-tall parent. (The even larger emperor penguin breeds on sea ice in the dead of winter, and was never seen on our cruises.)

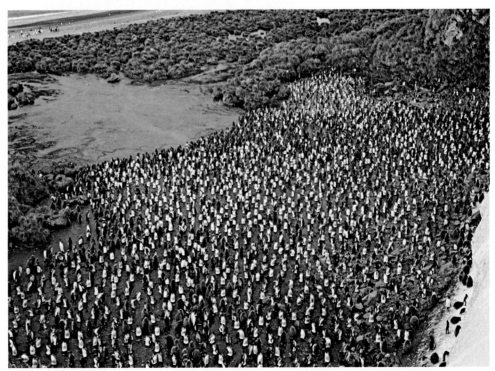

From left—The 30-inch-tall Adelie is recognized by its solid black head and white eye-ring. An adult watches the first of its two eggs hatch. Immature Adelies are gathered in a nursery supervised by adults, where the feeding grounds become filthy with krill.

Opposite—The most mind-boggling penguin colony of them all. Hundreds of thousands of Adelies breed here at Cape Adare each summer, as well as all around the rim of the continent and on the islands offshore. The colony is in constant movement, the air full of raucous voices and fetid odors.

The yellow-eyed penguin breeds on subantarctic islands as far north as Stewart Island. They lay their two eggs under an isolated root or log.

Two macaroni penguins have climbed the rocks well above the gravel beach to find nesting space on Elephant Island. It has many colonies in the Atlantic sector of the subantarctic islands.

The beautiful crested royal penguin, considered by some to be the same species as the macaroni, nests only on Macquarie Island. Between 2 and 3 million birds come here each season, some walking up shallow streams to breeding colonies a quarter of a mile inland.

94

Magellan penguins live in colonies of millions on the Atlantic shore of southern Patagonia. They are the most numerous of the three stripe-faced South American penguins. Both the 28-inch-tall adults at far left and the two chicks are standing outside nesting burrows.

The beautiful royal albatross breeds principally on Campbell Island, coming every second year to the island's heights. This bird has been banded by New Zealand naturalists.

96

The strong South Georgia wind ruffles the down of an immature wandering albatross. It is about the size of a young turkey. Easily caught by sealers and whalers, it was "tastier than pullet."

Above—Every second year the black-browed albatross lays a single egg in a cup-shaped nest of peat and dry grass, which is used over and over again. *Below*—A sooty light-mantled albatross, nesting in the tussock grass on South Georgia.

The wandering albatross has a dignified profile, the beak here stained with peat used in building its nest. It incubates a single egg every second year.

A handsome gray-headed albatross nests in the tussock grass. It must be near powerful air currents to take off or land.

97

Right—A giant petrel nests on a few stones on King George Island. These birds skim their food from the sea.

Top—A snow petrel, the only all-white member of its large family, nests on a small rock ledge of Signy Island. *Bottom*—Pintado (painted) petrels are called cape pigeons and nest in large numbers on Signy Island.

Left top—A blue-eyed shag defends its tall cupped nest by spreading its wings and ruffling its feathers.
Bottom—Sheathbills are the scavengers of antarctic beaches, cleaning up dead or dying penguin chicks, eggshells and food spilled in regurgitation.

Skuas are predatory gulls whose chief food is penguins. At top, a brown skua tears at a penguin carcass, and below, an Adelie penguin looks on unmoved as a MacCormick skua feasts on a dead Adelie.

99

The king, above, and the emperor, below, are the largest penguins.

Left to right: rockhopper, yellow-eyed, gentoo, chinstrap, Magellan.

Appendix A
CHRONOLOGY

1772-1775	Captain James Cook, British explorer, first crosses the polar circle, circumnavigates Antarctica, but sees no land.
1820	Captains Edward Bransfield, Royal Navy, and Nathaniel Palmer, Connecticut sealer; and Admiral von Bellingshausen, Imperial Russian Navy, all sight the continent, but do not land.
1822-1823	Captain James Weddell, British sealer, discovers Weddell Sea and brings home a Weddell seal.
1895	Norwegian-Australian Carstens Borchgrevink is first to land on the continent, and in 1898, first to winter on land.
1901-1904	Captain Robert Falcon Scott, Royal Navy, spends two winters on McMurdo Sound exploring coast and, with Sir Ernest Shackleton and Dr. E. A. Wilson, the Ross Ice Shelf.
1907-1909	Sir Ernest Shackleton, British, makes first attempt to reach South Pole, and nearly succeeds. Other members of party climb Mount Erebus and locate south magnetic pole.
December 14, 1911	Captain Roald Amundsen reaches South Pole.
January 17, 1912	Captain Robert Scott reaches South Pole. His party perishes on the return trip.
1914-1916	Sir Ernest Shackleton attempts first crossing of Antarctica. Ship crushed, the party makes remarkable survival journey.
1928-1929	Sir Hubert Wilkins, Australian, makes first flights in Antarctica, in extensive exploration.
November 29, 1929	Rear Admiral Richard E. Byrd flies over South Pole.
1933-1938	Lincoln Ellsworth, American, makes trans-Antarctic flight and extensive air exploration.
1939-1943	Admiral Sir James Clark Ross, Royal Navy, discovers Ross Sea, Island and Ice Shelf.
1946-1947	Operation Highjump. Byrd directs extensive aerial mapping.
1954-1956	Operation Deep Freeze. U.S. preparation for International Geophysical Year.
1957-1958	International Geophysical Year.
December 1, 1959	Antarctic Treaty signed, to go into force in 1961 for a period of 30 years.

Few people have seen all 17 species of penguin, which are scattered from the Galapagos archipelago to the continent of Antarctica. Most inhabit the subantarctic islands. Only four are found on the continent itself: the emperor, gentoo, chinstrap, and—best-known and most-studied of the group—the familiar tuxedo-clad Adelie. (The others: rockhopper, jackass, yellow-eyed, Snares crested, Fiordland crested, Magellan, macaroni, royal, Galapagos, Peruvian, king, erect-crested, little blue.)

All penguins are flightless, with wings resembling flippers, which they use to fly underwater at speeds up to 16 knots. Their dense feathers look more like scales. Penguins feed on krill or small fish and are often agile enough in water to evade their traditional predators, leopard seals and killer whales. Contrary to their popular image, their survival in this harsh environment is anything but comical.

Sizes range from the impressive 4-foot emperor and the 3-foot king to the 16-inch little blue penguin of Australia. The other species are from 18 to 30 inches in height. Probably the Adelie is the most numerous, nesting in colonies of millions on the rim of Antarctica. While there are only about 4,000 Galapagos penguins, they have never been numerous and are not under pressure; the Peruvian of coastal Chile and Peru is the most endangered species.

Nesting habits vary. The emperor breeds on sea ice off Antarctica in winter. While the females return to sea to fatten, the males huddle in a tight mass, each holding one egg on top of its feet. Females return at hatching time and take over.

At the other extreme are species that nest in burrows or in isolated nooks under roots in the coastal forests of New Zealand. The common image, of course, is the Adelie, nesting on pebbles in its mind-boggling colonies.

Appendix B

TEXT OF THE ANTARCTIC TREATY OF 1st DECEMBER 1959

A final Act of the Conference on the Antarctic and the Antarctic Treaty were signed at Washington on 1st December 1959. The texts were subsequently published as a United Kingdom Government White Paper (Cmnd. 913) from which the following text is taken.

The Antarctic Treaty

The Governments of Argentina, Australia, Belgium, Chile, the French Republic, Japan, New Zealand, Norway, the Union of South Africa, the Union of Soviet Socialist Republics, the United Kingdom of Great Britain and Northern Ireland, and the United States of America.

Recognising that it is in the interest of all mankind that the Antarctic shall continue for ever to be used exclusively for peaceful purposes and shall not become the scene or object of international discord;

Acknowledging the substantial contributions to scientific knowledge resulting from international co-operation in scientific investigation in the Antarctic;

Convinced that the establishment of a firm foundation for the continuation and development of such co-operation on the basis of freedom of scientific investigation in the Antarctic as applied during the International Geophysical Year accords with the interests of science and the progress of all mankind;

Convinced also that a treaty ensuring the use of the Antarctic for peaceful purposes only and the continuance of international harmony in the Antarctic will further the purposes and principles embodied in the Charter of the United Nations;

Have agreed as follows:

Article I

1. The Antarctic shall be used for peaceful purposes only. There shall be prohibited, *inter alia*, any measures of a military nature, such as the establishment of military bases and fortifications, the carrying out of military manoeuvres, as well as the testing of any type of weapons.
2. The present Treaty shall not prevent the use of military personnel or equipment for scientific research or for any other peaceful purpose.

Article II

Freedom of scientific investigation in the Antarctic and co-operation toward that end, as applied during the International Geophysical Year, shall continue, subject to the provisions of the present Treaty.

Article III

1. In order to promote international co-operation in scientific investigation in the Antarctic, as provided for in Article II of the present Treaty, the Contracting Parties agree that, to the greatest extent feasible and practicable:

   (a) information regarding plans for scientific programmes in the Antarctic shall be exchanged to permit maximum economy and efficiency of operations;

   (b) scientific personnel shall be exchanged in the Antarctic between expeditions and stations;

   (c) scientific observations and results from the Antarctic shall be exchanged and made freely available.

Adelie.

Little blue.

2. In implementing this Article, every encouragement shall be given to the establishment of co-operative working relations with those Specialised Agencies of the United Nations and other international organisations having a scientific or technical interest in the Antarctic.

Article IV

1. Nothing contained in the present Treaty shall be interpreted as:

(a) a renunciation by any Contracting Party of previously asserted rights of or claims to territorial sovereignty in the Antarctic;

(b) a renunciation or diminution by any Contracting Party of any basis of claim to territorial sovereignty in the Antarctic which it may have whether as a result of its activities or those of its nationals in the Antarctic, or otherwise;

(c) prejudicing the position of any Contracting Party as regards its recognition or non-recognition of any other State's right of or claim or basis of claim to territorial sovereignty in the Antarctic.

2. No acts or activities taking place while the present Treaty is in force shall constitute a basis for asserting, supporting or denying a claim to territorial sovereignty in the Antarctic or create any rights of sovereignty in the Antarctic. No new claim, or enlargement of an existing claim, to territorial sovereignty in the Antarctic shall be asserted while the present Treaty is in force.

Article V

1. Any nuclear explosions in the Antarctic and the disposal there of radioactive waste material shall be prohibited.

2. In the event of the conclusion of international agreements concerning the use of nuclear energy, including nuclear explosions and the disposal of radioactive waste material, to which all of the Contracting Parties whose representatives are entitled to participate in the meetings provided for under Article IX are parties, the rules established under such agreements shall apply in the Antarctic.

Article VI

The provision of the present Treaty shall apply to the area south of 60° South Latitude, including all ice shelves, but nothing in the present Treaty shall prejudice or in any way affect the rights, or the exercise of the rights, of any State under international law with regard to the high seas within that area.

Article VII

1. In order to promote the objectives and ensure the observance of the provisions of the present Treaty, each Contracting Party whose representatives are entitled to participate in the meetings referred to in Article IX of the Treaty shall have the right to designate observers to carry out any inspection provided for by the present Article. Observers shall be nationals of the Contracting Parties which designate them. The names of observers shall be communicated to every other Contracting Party having the right to designate observers, and like notice shall be given of the termination of their appointment.

2. Each observer designated in accordance with the provisions of paragraph 1 of this Article shall have complete freedom of access at any time to any or all areas of the Antarctic.

3. All areas of the Antarctic, including all stations, installations and equipment within those areas, and all ships and aircraft at points of discharging or embarking cargoes or personnel in the Antarctic, shall be open at all times to inspection by any observers designated in accordance with paragraph 1 of this Article.

4. Aerial observation may be carried out at any time over any or all areas of the Antarctic by any of the Contracting Parties having the right to designate observers.

5. Each Contracting Party shall, at the time when the present Treaty enters into force, inform the other Contracting Parties, and thereafter shall give them notice in advance, of

(a) all expeditions to and within the Antarctic, on the part of its ships or nationals, and all expeditions to the Antarctic organised in or proceeding from its territory;

(b) all stations in the Antarctic occupied by its nationals; and

(c) any military personnel or equipment intended to be introduced by it into the Antarctic subject to the conditions prescribed in paragraph 2 of Article I of the present Treaty.

Article VIII

1. In order to facilitate the exercise of their functions under the

present Treaty, and without prejudice to the respective positions of the Contracting Parties relating to jurisdiction over all other persons in the Antarctic, observers designated under paragraph 1 of Article VII and scientific personnel exchanged under subparagraph 1 (b) of Article III of the Treaty, and members of the staffs accompanying any such persons, shall be subject only to the jurisdiction of the Contracting Party of which they are nationals in respect of all acts or omissions occurring while they are in the Antarctic for the purpose of exercising their functions.

2. Without prejudice to the provisions of paragraph 1 of this Article, and pending the adoption of measures in pursuance of subparagraph 1 (e) of Article IX, the Contracting Parties concerned in any case of dispute with regard to the exercise of jurisdiction in the Antarctic shall immediately consult together with a view to reaching a mutually acceptable solution.

Article IX

1. Representatives of the Contracting Parties named in the preamble to the present Treaty shall meet at the City of Canberra within two months after the date of entry into force of the Treaty, and thereafter at suitable intervals and places, for the purpose of exchanging information, consulting together on matters of common interest pertaining to the Antarctic, and formulating and considering, and recommending to their governments, measures in furtherance of the principles and objectives of the Treaty, including measures regarding:

(a) use of the Antarctic for peaceful purposes only;

(b) facilitation of scientific research in the Antarctic;

(c) facilitation of international scientific co-operation in the Antarctic;

(d) facilitation of the exercise of the rights of inspection provided for in Article VII of the Treaty;

(e) questions relating to the exercise of jurisdiction in the Antarctic;

(f) preservation and conservation of living resources in the Antarctic.

2. Each Contracting Party which has become a party to the present Treaty by accession under Article XIII shall be entitled to appoint representatives to participate in the meetings referred to in paragraph 1 of the present Article, during such time as that Contracting Party demonstrates its interest in the Antarctic by conducting substantial scientific research activity there, such as the establishment of a scientific station or the dispatch of a scientific expedition.

3. Reports from the observers referred to in Article VII of the present Treaty shall be transmitted to the representatives of the Contracting Parties participating in the meetings referred to in paragraph 1 of the present Article.

4. The measures referred to in paragraph 1 of this Article shall become effective when approved by all the Contracting Parties whose representatives were entitled to participate in the meetings held to consider those measures.

5. Any or all of the rights established in the present Treaty may be exercised as from the date of entry into force of the Treaty whether or not any measures facilitating the exercise of such rights have been proposed, considered or approved as provided in this Article.

Article X

Each of the Contracting Parties undertakes to exert appropriate efforts, consistent with the Charter of the United Nations, to the end that no one engages in any activity in the Antarctic contrary to the principles or purposes of the present Treaty.

Article XI

1. If any dispute arises between two or more of the Contracting Parties concerning the interpretation or application of the present Treaty, those Contracting Parties shall consult among themselves with a view to having the dispute resolved by negotiation, inquiry, mediation, conciliation, arbitration, judicial settlement or other peaceful means of their own choice.

2. Any dispute of this character not so resolved shall, with the consent, in each case, of all parties to the dispute, be referred to the International Court of Justice for settlement; but failure to reach agreement on reference to the International Court shall not absolve parties to the dispute from the responsibility of continuing to seek to resolve it by any of the various peaceful means referred to in paragraph 1 of this Article.

Article XII

1. (a) The present Treaty may be modified or amended at any time by unanimous agreement of the Contracting Parties whose representatives are entitled to participate in the meetings provided for under Article IX. Any such modification or amendment shall enter into force when the depositary

Government has received notice from all such Contracting Parties that they have ratified it.

(b) Such modification or amendment shall thereafter enter into force as to any other Contracting Party when notice of ratification by it has been received by the depositary Government. Any such Contracting Party from which no notice of ratification is received within a period of two years from the date of entry into force of the modification or amendment in accordance with the provisions of subparagraph 1 (a) of this Article shall be deemed to have withdrawn from the present Treaty on the date of the expiration of such period.

2. (a) If after the expiration of thirty years from the date of entry into force of the present Treaty, any of the Contracting Parties whose representatives are entitled to participate in the meetings provided for under Article IX so requests by a communication addressed to the depositary Government, a Conference of all the Contracting Parties shall be held as soon as practicable to review the operation of the Treaty.

(b) Any modification or amendment to the present Treaty which is approved at such a Conference by a majority of the Contracting Parties there represented, including a majority of those whose representatives are entitled to participate in the meetings provided for under Article IX, shall be communicated by the depositary Government to all the Contracting Parties immediately after the termination of the Conference and shall enter into force in accordance with the provisions of paragraph 1 of the present Article.

(c) If any such modification or amendment has not entered into force in accordance with the provisions of subparagraph 1 (a) of this Article within a period of two years after the date of its communication to all the Contracting Parties, any Contracting Party may at any time after the expiration of that period give notice to the depositary Government of its withdrawal from the present Treaty; and such withdrawal shall take effect two years after the receipt of the notice by the depositary Government.

Article XIII

1. The present Treaty shall be subject to ratification by the signatory States. It shall be open for accession by any State which is a Member of the United Nations, or by any other State which may be invited to accede to the Treaty with the consent of all the Contracting Parties whose representatives are entitled to participate in the meetings provided for under Article IX of the Treaty.

2. Ratification of or accession to the present Treaty shall be effected by each State in accordance with its constitutional processes.

3. Instruments of ratification and instruments of accession shall be deposited with the Government of the United States of America, hereby designated as the depositary Government.

4. The depositary Government shall inform all signatory and acceding States of the date of each deposit of an instrument of ratification or accession, and the date of entry into force of the Treaty and of any modification or amendment thereto.

5. Upon the deposit of instruments of ratification by all the signatory States, the present Treaty shall enter into force for those States and for States which have deposited instruments of accession. Thereafter the Treaty shall enter into force for any acceding State upon the deposit of its instrument of accession.

Article XIV

The present Treaty, done in the English, French, Russian, and Spanish languages, each version being equally authentic, shall be deposited in the archives of the Government of the United States of America, which shall transmit duly certified copies thereof to the Governments of the signatory and acceding States.

IN WITNESS WHEREOF, the undersigned Plenipotentiaries, duly authorised, have signed the present Treaty.

DONE at Washington this first day of December one thousand nine hundred and fifty-nine.

[Here follow the signatures on behalf of the Governments of: Argentina, Australia, Belgium, Chile, France, Japan, New Zealand, Norway, Union of South Africa, Union of Soviet Socialist Republics, United Kingdom of Great Britain and Northern Ireland, United States of America.] ◄◄◄